25 Christmas Myths
and what the Bible says

GABRIEL HUGHES

WWUTT
When We Understand the Text

For best results, read with your Bible open. Why not begin with Matthew 1-2 and Luke 1-2?

Table of Contents

Myth #1
Jesus was born on December 25.

Christmas is an annual holiday commemorating the birth of Jesus Christ, the Son of God and promised Messiah, who came into our world as a baby born in Bethlehem over 2,000 years ago. Every year on December 25th, billions of people around the globe celebrate Christmas with worship, music, gifts, food, décor, lights, stories, and festivities. No other holiday, not even among the seasonal solstices and equinoxes, is as woven into so many cultures or endeared to so many people as Christmas Day.

Christmas comes with many fond memories for my family and me. Perhaps it does for you as well. But not everything is peace on earth and goodwill towards men. The commercialization of Christmas can suck the joy right out of things. For some, the holidays are a time of stress, anxiety, and depression. The beauty of the gospel in the Christmas story has been shrouded by myth, legend, and paganism. Meanwhile, cynics clamor every year to defrock Christmas of its religious heritage and make the season more secular.

Indeed, Christmas has its share of Scrooges, Grinches, and Herods. But no one can change the fact that Christmas has been and will continue to be a Christian tradition for generations. We live in a fallen world. Not all was calm and bright on that first Christmas either — which we'll consider further as we open the Scriptures and examine the specifics of the first advent of Jesus.

Yes, Christmas can be a wonderful time with friends and family, experiencing all the warmth the holiday season makes us feel. But at the heart of the Christmas story is the truth that all of humanity is fallen from God because of our sin, and God sent us a Savior. In all our Christmas celebrations should be the message of the gospel: "Christ Jesus came into the world to save sinners" (1 Timothy 1:15).

Now, just because Christmas Day is a celebration of the birth of Christ, that doesn't mean Jesus was born on that day. How December 25th became the birthdate of Jesus is difficult to trace, but it did not come from the Bible. The Scriptures do not tell us on exactly what day Jesus was born. Only two of the four gospels detail the events around His birth, and there's no mention in the rest of the New Testament of anyone celebrating His birthday.

The earliest church writers like Irenaeus (130-200 AD) and Tertullian (160-225 AD) made no comment on an official observance of Christ's birth. In fact,

Origen of Alexandria (165-264 AD) mocked the idea of celebrating birthdays at all. He wrote, "Of all the holy people in the Scriptures, no one is recorded to have kept a feast or held a great banquet on his birthday. It is only sinners (like Pharaoh and Herod) who make great rejoicings over the day on which they were born into this world below."[1]

The most widely accepted theory is that Roman Emperor Constantine had Christianized an existing pagan holiday. In 274 A.D., Emperor Aurelian—who persecuted Christians and declared he was a god—chose December 25th as the birthdate of Sol Invictus, the god of the unconquerable sun. But then in 336, Constantine changed December 25th to the birthdate of Jesus Christ. No longer a celebration of the birth of the *sun*, it became a celebration of the birth of the *Son!* Get it?

But that's also a myth. There's no proof Emperor Constantine chose December 25th as the birthdate of Christ. While Constantine often gets far too much credit for a lot of Christian traditions, does anyone ever question why Aurelian chose December 25th as the birthdate of the sun in the first place? The winter solstice was on December 21st, the day the sun died according to pagan tradition. Aurelian may have thought of the sun being dead for three days—the 22nd, 23rd, and 24th—and then it came back to life on the 25th. *Now where would he get that idea from?*

---

[1] Origen, *Homilies on Leviticus,* Homily 8.

7

About 40 years before Aurelian dedicated his temple to the Roman sun god, Hippolytus of Rome (170-235 AD) wrote in a commentary on Daniel that he believed Jesus was born on the 25th of December.[2] Before Hippolytus, Clement of Alexandria (150-215 AD) believed Jesus was born on the 6th of January.[3] December 25 eventually won out as the popular date of Christ's birth, while January 6 became known as Epiphany — a celebration of the day the Magi visited the Christ child. (The twelve days between these two dates is where the twelve days of Christmas come from.)

After Jesus died on the cross for our sins, He was buried in a tomb and then came back to life three days later. Is that where Aurelian got his idea for the death and resurrection of his sun god? I'm not saying it is or isn't. What I will say is this: if one wants to

---

[2] Hippolytus, *Commentary on Daniel*, Book 4, 23:3, "For the first advent of our Lord in the flesh, when he was born in Bethlehem, was December 25th [eight days before the Kalends of January], Wednesday [the fourth day], while Augustus was in his forty-second year, but from Adam, five thousand and five hundred years. He suffered in the thirty-third year, March 25th [eight days before the Kalends of March], Friday [the Day of Preparation], the eighteenth year of Tiberius Caesar, while Rufus and Roubellion were Consuls."

[3] Beckwith, Roger T. Brill. *Calendar and Chronology, Jewish and Christian: Biblical, Intertestamental, and Patristic Studies.* 2001. Pg. 72-73.

argue that a celebration of Christ's birth was meant to replace a pagan holiday, one could just as easily make the argument that a pagan holiday was meant to replace a day remembering Christ's birth. The Christian tradition that December 25th is the birthday of Jesus precedes any pagan tradition that December 25th was the birthday of a false god.

Perhaps this explains how December 25th became the accepted day of the birth of Christ. But it still doesn't mean we know on what actual day He was born. That's an answer we may never know with certainty this side of heaven.

It's possible Jesus was born around December 25th and January 6th. Who's to say Hippo and Clem didn't know something we don't? The reason we attack those dates as mythical is because we've come to believe the myth that Christmas swiped a pagan holiday. Rather than pay mind to speculation, let us consider what the text says. In Luke 2:8-14, we read:

> And in the same region, there were shepherds out in the field, keeping watch over their flock by night. And an angel of the Lord appeared to them, and the glory of the Lord shone around them, and they were filled with great fear.
>
> And the angel said to them, "Fear not, for behold I bring you good news of great joy that will be for all the people. For unto you is born this day in the city of David a Savior, who is

Christ the Lord. And this will be a sign for you: you will find a baby wrapped in swaddling cloths and lying in a manger."

And suddenly there was with the angel a multitude of the heavenly host, praising God and saying, "Glory to God in the highest, and on earth peace among those with whom He is pleased."

Because of what is said in Luke 2:8, most scholars believe it is unlikely that Jesus was born in winter. Notice first that the shepherds were "out in the field." Shepherds took their flocks out to the field after the wheat and barley had been harvested, which would have been from late spring to before late autumn. The sheep and goats would eat the grain that had fallen to the harvest floor and any extra grass or cut stalks. The fields would then be plowed and planted for the next year's crop.

Secondly, the shepherds kept "watch over their flock by night." Only in summer, or the dry season, were sheep pastured in the fields. Flocks grazed closer to home during the wet season which went from November to March.[4] At night, the sheep and goats were brought in and separated out into folds

---

[4] Crabre, Addison Darre. *The Journeys of Jesus: A Chronological, Geographical, and Topographical History of the Journeys of Jesus and the Twelve Disciples in Palestine* (Palestine Publishing Company, 1884). Pg. 44.

and pens where they would be protected from any predators.

So there's no way Jesus was born on December 25th, right? Keep in mind that in Judea, shepherding was a year-round occupation. The shepherds were tending the sheep used for sacrifices in the temple. Sheep need to eat in December, too, and it would not have been too cold for shepherds to be out with them by night. To this day, shepherds are indeed out in the field "keeping watch over their flock by night," even on December 25th.

Then on what day was Jesus born? Again, God only knows. In what year was he born? The year 0, right? After all, the Gregorian calendar system that we use today separates eras into B.C., or the years Before Christ, and A.D., or *Anno Domini* which is Latin for "in the year of the Lord" (not "After Death," as is often assumed). Therefore, Jesus had to have been born in the year 0, and everything before that happened "before Christ."

Well, there isn't a year 0. The calendar rolls over from 1 B.C. to 1 A.D. (which is why some calendar purists argue that the twenty-first century officially began in the year 2001, not in the year 2000). *Anno Domini* was devised in the year 525 by Dionysius Exiguus, a Scythian monk who lived in Rome. Until he came up with this dating label, calendar years were identified by the name of whatever Roman consul held office in the year being referenced.

When Dionysius first used *Anno Domini*, he was trying to avoid naming years marked by emperors who persecuted Christians, particularly Diocletian. It wasn't until the eighth century that it caught on, when the Venerable Bede used *Anno Domini* in his work *The Ecclesiastical History of the English People.* The Gregorian calendar system officially replaced the Julian calendar system in 1582 under Pope Gregory XIII.

Unfortunately, Dionysius wasn't trying to be terribly precise with his dating—he was just trying to avoid using Diocletian's name. *Anno Domini* happens to be a few years off, and it's unlikely that Jesus was born in either 1 B.C. or 1 A.D.

In Matthew 2, when the Magi came to visit Jesus, Herod the Great was king in Jerusalem. The common belief is that Herod's reign began in 37 B.C. until he died in 4 B.C.—this according to the Jewish historian Josephus. Therefore, Jesus could not have been born in 1 B.C., for that would have been three years after Herod's death. Rather, Jesus may have been born in 5 or 6 B.C. since He would have been under two years of age at the time the Magi arrived in Bethlehem (see Matthew 2:16). We'll examine these dates and events more thoroughly later.

No matter the discrepancies, it's amazing to consider that the most widely used calendar system in the world is based around the life of Jesus. After all, Philippians 2:9 says that God has "bestowed on

Him the name that is above every name." Secularists have attempted to stifle the truth by changing B.C. and A.D. to B.C.E. and C.E., standing for "before the common era" and "common era" respectively. This is nothing but semantics. It still doesn't change the fact that the very year in which we live was calculated according to the time it is understood that Jesus came to earth—or as John 1:14 puts it, "The Word became flesh and dwelt among us."

No event in the history of the world has been more important than the birth, life, death, and resurrection of Jesus Christ. A reminder of His first coming is commemorated on your calendar every year—Christmas Day, December 25th.

REFLECTION
Think about which Christmas Day was your favorite Christmas that you have celebrated. What made that particular Christmas so special to you? Did you have a relationship with Jesus? How did your worship of God play a role in making that Christmas special? If you are reading this as a family, sing a couple verses of the hymn *The First Noel*. Here are the lyrics:[5]

> *The first Noel the angel did say,*
> *Was to certain poor shepherds*
> *In fields as they lay;*

---

[5] "The First Noel" (*Hymns of Grace*; The Master's Seminary Press; Los Angeles, CA; 2015). Hymn 223.

In fields where they lay keeping their sheep,
On a cold winter's night that was so deep.
Noel, Noel, Noel, Noel,
Born is the King of Israel!

Then let us all with one accord
Sing praises to our heavenly Lord
Who hath made heaven and earth of naught,
And with His blood mankind He hath bought.
Noel, Noel, Noel, Noel,
Born is the King of Israel!

Myth #2

Mary wasn't married when she became pregnant.

In Luke 1:28-38, God sent the angel Gabriel to Nazareth, a city of Galilee, to appear "to a virgin betrothed to a man whose name was Joseph, of the house of David. And the virgin's name was Mary."

Gabriel said to Mary, "Greetings, O favored one, the Lord is with you!" But Mary was stricken with fear. The angel said, "Do not be afraid, Mary, for you have found favor with God. And behold, you will conceive in your womb and bear a son, and you shall call His name Jesus. He will be great and will be called the Son of the Most High. And the Lord God will give to Him the throne of His father David, and He will reign over the house of Jacob forever, and of His kingdom there will be no end."

Mary said to the angel, "How will this be, since I am a virgin?"

The angel answered her, "The Holy Spirit will come upon you, and the power of the Most High will overshadow you; therefore the child to be born will be called holy — the Son of God."

One of the most famous Christmas songs, if not one of the most famous of any song in the world, is *Silent Night.* Every Christmas, it is sung the world over:

Silent night, holy night,
All is calm, all is bright.
Round yon virgin, mother and child.
Holy infant so tender and mild.[6]

Surely everyone who has heard of Christmas also knows the story of the virgin Mary who gave birth to the baby Jesus. Since Mary was a virgin when she was found to be with child, she couldn't have been married, right? After all, if Mary and Joseph were married, they would have already consummated their relationship, and she would not have been a virgin anymore.

Truth be told, Mary and Joseph *were* married, but they had not yet consummated their marriage (or as it is often joked, Joseph had not yet known his wife *biblically*). In fact, when it became known that Mary was pregnant, Joseph wanted to divorce her. Here is what we read in Matthew 1:18-25:

Now the birth of Jesus Christ took place in this way. When His mother Mary had been

---

[6] Mohr, Joseph. "Silent Night, Holy Night" *(Hymns of Grace).* Hymn 236.

betrothed to Joseph, before they came together, she was found to be with child from the Holy Spirit. And her husband Joseph, being a just man and unwilling to put her to shame, resolved to divorce her quietly. But as he considered these things, behold, an angel of the Lord appeared to him in a dream, saying, "Joseph, son of David, do not fear to take Mary as your wife, for that which is conceived in her is from the Holy Spirit. She will bear a son, and you shall call His name Jesus, for He will save His people from their sins."

All this took place to fulfill what the Lord had spoken by the prophet: "Behold, the virgin shall conceive and bear a son, and they shall call His name Immanuel" (which means God with us).

When Joseph woke from sleep, he did as the angel of the Lord commanded him: he took his wife, but knew her not until she had given birth to a son. And he called His name Jesus.

The misunderstanding related to Mary's status as *betrothed* is a cultural one. In our modern, western society, marriage is often preceded by engagement. While a marriage is legally binding, an engagement is not. One or both parties may end an engagement at any time without there being much fuss (where the law is concerned anyway).

The word *betrothed* is not terribly common in our culture. If and when we refer to the *betrothed*, it's often in the context of an engagement, and it can apply to either a man or a woman. A fiancée might refer to her fiancé as her betrothed, and that means they are promised to be married. She's got a ring, they've made the announcement, they've sent out save-the-date cards ahead of the invitations, then they sent out the invitations themselves, there are showers, parties, photo-shoots, the caterer has been booked, the venue has been scheduled, the colors have been selected, dresses tried on, china pattern chosen, stores registered — *lots of money* will be spent. But the couple is still not legally obligated to one another until the wedding happens and the marriage license has been signed and issued.

In a first century Jewish culture, more emphasis was put on the marriage than the wedding. If a woman was betrothed, she was legally bound to a man as his wife. She spent that betrothal period learning how to be a wife, and he spent that time establishing his livelihood and preparing a house in which to raise a family. The marriage would not be consummated (to put it bluntly, sex wasn't involved) until after the wedding, and the wife moved into the home her husband had prepared.

Arranged marriages were common — a father could give a daughter to be married with or without her consent. Between Joseph and Mary, likely they caught one another's eye, he expressed to Mary a desire to be wed, and Mary told her father that she wanted to be Joseph's wife. Joseph met with Mary's father, some exchange of oaths or goods took place, and Mary was legally promised to Joseph and no other man. They were, for all intents and purposes, *married.*

Now, lest you think Mary was regarded as property or subjected to some joyless servitude, she loved Joseph and wanted to be his wife. This was an exciting time for a young woman, likely between 14 and 17 years of age. During her betrothal, which would have lasted about a year, Mary may have lived with Joseph's family and worked with the other married women, learning how to be a wife and raise children. According to the tradition of that time, a man commonly chose a bride from within his own tribe, so their two families were related by lineage, and they were close.

Joseph practiced the trade of his father, which we know to be carpentry (Matthew 13:55). We might think of a carpenter as someone who builds with wood, but in first century Palestine, that would have included any local building material, whether wood, stone, or metal. Every town had a master-builder who would supervise all building projects for that community and the surrounding villages. Joseph had assumed that responsibility from his father, and Jesus would have worked that job as well (in Mark 6:3, Jesus is called "the carpenter" in Nazareth, His hometown).

As was the custom for all bridegrooms, Joseph had the responsibility of preparing a home for his bride, while Mary learned to tend to her household. Included in this preparation was the setting of a room where Joseph and Mary would consummate their marriage, and these two persons from different families would become one flesh forming one new family.

Jesus referenced this custom with His disciples, using wedding language to describe His relationship with His followers. "In my Father's house are many rooms," He said. "If it were not so, would I have told you that I go to prepare a place for you? And if I go and prepare a place for you, I will come again and will take you to myself that where I am you may be also" (John 14:3-4).

Even now, the church is called the bride of Christ, and Christ is our bridegroom (Mark 2:19, John 3:29, Ephesians 5:22-33, Revelation 18:23, 21:9). Our union with Christ has not yet been consummated. This will not happen until Christ returns and receives His own. In Revelation 19:7, we read, "Let us rejoice and exult and give Him the glory, for the marriage of the Lamb has come, and His Bride has made herself ready." Then we will all be gathered for the marriage supper of the Lamb (Revelation 19:6-10).

We are in this moment Christ's betrothed. We are His bride, legally promised to Christ, sealed by a covenant, though we have not yet come into the dwelling place that He is preparing for us. So this was the case also with Joseph and Mary. At the time Mary became with child, she was married to Joseph, though their union had not yet been consummated.

Again, Matthew 1:19 reads, "And her *husband* Joseph, being a just man and unwilling to put her to shame, resolved to divorce her quietly." Here Joseph is described as her husband, and to separate from Mary would have been to divorce her. He would have given her a certificate of divorce breaking their marriage covenant.

Under the law, unfaithfulness was a permissible reason for divorce. Joseph knew he wasn't the father of the child Mary was expecting, so logically he believed that she had been unfaithful. Being a just man, he wanted to keep the law of God, so he resolved to divorce Mary, and decided to do this quietly. He knew that if she'd been unfaithful, the law was already on his side. There was no reason to justify himself further by making a spectacle of her.

But an angel spoke to him in a dream and said, "Joseph, son of David, do not fear to take Mary as your wife, for that which is conceived in her is from the Holy Spirit. She will bear a son, and you shall call His name Jesus, for He will save His people from their sins."

Of course, we know Joseph decided to remain with Mary, but he never knew her—*biblically*—until after Jesus was born. Joseph was a strong man, several years older than Mary, capable of taking care of his young virgin wife and the Christ child. It was a marriage arranged not by an earthly father, but by our Heavenly Father.

REFLECTION

If you are studying this book together as a family, sing these verses of *Silent Night*. Here are the lyrics:

> *Silent night, holy night,*
> *All is calm, all is bright.*
> *Round yon virgin, mother and child.*
> *Holy infant so tender and mild.*
> *Sleep in heavenly peace.*
> *Sleep in heavenly peace.*
>
> *Silent night, holy night,*
> *Shepherds quake at the sight.*
> *Glories stream from heaven afar,*
> *Heavenly hosts sing: "Allelujah!*
> *Christ the Savior is born,*
> *Christ the Savior is born."*
>
> *Silent night, holy night*
> *Son of God, love's pure light*
> *Radiant beams from Thy holy face,*
> *With the dawn of redeeming grace,*
> *Jesus, Lord, at Thy birth,*
> *Jesus, Lord at Thy birth.*

What is the difference between *heavenly peace* and an earthly peace? How does knowing Jesus is Lord give you peace? How can understanding that God has all our circumstances in His hands bring comfort to your soul?

Myth #3

The gospel of Luke is wrong about the census.

Luke 2:1-5 says, "In those days, a decree went out from Caesar Augustus that all the world should be registered. This was the first registration when Quirinius was governor of Syria. And all went to be registered, each to his own town. And Joseph also went up from Galilee, from the town of Nazareth, to Judea, to the city of David which is called Bethlehem, because he was of the house and lineage of David, to be registered with Mary, his betrothed, who was with child."

Growing up, I never knew there were any doubts about this passage. My dad read it and explained it to my siblings and me every Christmas. I heard it read in every Christmas cantata and Christmas Eve service I attended. I had no reason to question it. As the old saying goes, *"The Bible says it, that settles it."* Not until I attended college did I learn from friends and my professors that Luke's account of the birth of Christ is apparently fraught with problems.

As one university professor wrote, "There is no

record of Caesar Augustus' decree that 'all the world should be enrolled' (Lk. 2:1). The Romans kept extremely detailed records of such events. Not only is Luke's census not in these records, it goes against all that we know of Roman economic history. Roman documents show that taxation was done by the various governors at the provincial level... Property tax was collected on site by traveling assessors, thus making unnecessary Joseph's journey away from what little property he must have owned."[7]

Yes, the Romans kept excellent records, but we have not retained all those records. According to ancient historian and classical scholar Tenney Frank, "The census figures for Rome are given for almost every lustrum," or every five years. But after the reigns of emperors Tiberius and Gaius in the second century B.C., "the census was not always taken, and sometimes the statistics have been lost to us."[8]

Frank showed that during the time of Augustus, three censuses were taken, and rather than being taken every lustrum, these censuses were all ten or more years apart. It's reasonable to believe there was another census or two in there we simply don't have record of.

---

[7] Gier, N.F. *God, Reason, and the Evangelicals* (University Press of America, Lanham, MD; 1987). Pg. 145-146. https:// www.webpages.uidaho.edu/ngier/census.htm
[8] Frank, Tenney; *Classical Philology*, Vol. 19, No. 4, Roman Census Statistics from 225 to 28 B.C. (The University of Chicago Press, October, 1924). Pg. 331.

The most important information that was to be acquired from a Roman census was the registration of citizens and their property.[9] Contrary to what critics might say about Luke's account, some census decrees did require citizens to return to their homes.[10] This did not mean a mass movement of people since most landowners lived on or near their property. However, lands in Judea were often possessed by tribe or family.[11] Joseph would have gone to the place of his lineage to bear witness with the rest of his family regarding the lands that belonged to their tribe. We know that upon arriving in Bethlehem, Joseph and Mary lived with family (more regarding that in the next two chapters).

But these are not really the biggest problems critics have with Luke's story of the birth of Christ. As anyone with Google who can look up someone else who did all the research for their skepticism knows, the Jewish historian Josephus records that Quirinius wasn't governor of Syria until the year 6 A.D. King Herod the Great died in 4 B.C. The two

---

[9] Smith, William (editor); *A Dictionary of Greek and Roman Antiquities* (John Murray, London, 1875). Pg. 260-266. http://penelope.uchicago.edu/Thayer/E/Roman/Texts/secondary/SMIGRA/home.html

[10] Cobern, C.M. *The New Archeological Discoveries and Their Bearing Upon the New Testament* (Funk and Wagnalls, New York and London, 1929). Pg. 47.

[11] See Numbers 26:52-56, Joshua 13-22.

weren't even ruling at the same time! That means Luke is off by a whole decade! So the Bible is wrong! Show's over! Everyone pack up all your Christmas decorations and have a happy winter solstice!

But hang on—Why should we assume that the problem is with the biblical record? What if Josephus was wrong? *Gasp!*

Josephus wrote that Herod the Great was made king at the age of fifteen,[12] but scholars have rejected this erroneous claim as Herod was actually twenty-five. Why, that's a mistake of 10 years! Furthermore, Josephus says that Herod received the kingdom "having obtained it on the hundred eighty-fourth Olympiad; when Caius Domitius Calvinus was consul for the second time; and Caius Asinius Pollio for the first time."[13] But those consuls, Calvinus and Pollio, were not appointed until the hundred and eighty-*fifth* Olympiad.[14] Whoops!

Josephus was not some infallible historian. For years, scholars have been critical of the dates we've come to accept thanks to Josephus. Nevertheless, the traditional dates associated with the Christmas story

---

[12] Josephus, Flavius; *Antiquities of the Jews*, XIV 9:2.

[13] 7. Josephus, *Antiquities*, XIV 14:5. http://www.nowoez one.com/NTC04.html

[14] Edwards, Ormond. *Herodian Chronology; Palestine Exploration Quarterly* (1982). Volume 114, Pg. 29-42. https:// www.tandfonline.com/doi/abs/10.1179/peq.198 2.114.1.29?journalCode=ypeq20

remain the most popular. The only problem with the census in Luke 2 is that we try to make Luke's accurate record line up with inaccurate dates! Then he gets the blame when that doesn't work.

Perhaps you remain unconvinced by that answer. Then permit me to propose a much simpler solution to this riddle. You do not have to be a historian, understand Greek, or possess an encyclopedia of biblical archeology to grasp this explanation. All it takes is a careful analysis of the text.

Luke's gospel is addressed to a man named Theophilus: "It seemed good to me also, having followed all things closely for some time past, to write an orderly account for you, most excellent Theophilus, that you may have certainty concerning the things you have been taught" (Luke 1:3-4). That's the intended audience, and that's the reason for writing. The setting is in Judea, beginning in the days of Herod (v.5). Luke starts with the birth of John the Baptist, and then he tells of Gabriel's appearance to Mary, announcing that she will be with child.

Then we get to Luke 2:1 which begins, "In those days." That's quite unspecific. It's way more general than saying, *"In the same year of Christ's birth."* Luke then says, "a decree went out from Caesar Augustus that all the world should be registered." Again, we don't know exactly when this decree went out, or if such a registration was successfully completed in Judea when it was first issued.

The Jews had a rough history when it came to censuses. A thousand years earlier, King David, with pride, wanted to see how many people were in his kingdom. He ordered a census be taken despite wise objections from Joab, his most trusted official, who loathed the idea. David also did not follow the law of God when it came to the proper procedure for conducting a census in Israel.[15] Because of David's sin, God sent pestilence against the land, and 70,000 people died (2 Samuel 24:1-9, 1 Chronicles 21:1-17).

This was embedded in the history of the Jews, who refused to conduct a census unless God had commanded it. Add to this their contempt for the Romans. A group of Jews called the Zealots strongly opposed the Roman census. According to Acts 5:37 (which, by the way, was also written by Luke), Judas the Galilean "rose up in the days of the census" and rallied many people to follow him.

Though a census was decreed, it was not carried out in Judea without aggressive opposition. What census-taker wanted to risk their lives by going town to town counting people and their property? Caesar Augustus needed an enforcer, and Publius Sculpicius Quirinius, with his decorated war record, was just such a guy. Quirinius was made governor of Syria, and Judea, which had been unsuccessfully overseen by the Herods, was now brought under Quirinius' authority.

---

[15] See Exodus 30:11-16.

Luke 2:2 says, "This was the first registration when Quirinius was governor of Syria." All Luke was pointing out was that these events were part of the same drama. He was not saying that they all happened at the same time. Again, this was all "in those days" (v.1), which is an unspecific passing of time. Sometimes Luke does get very specific, as in Luke 3:1 where he says, "In the fifteenth year of the reign of Tiberius Caesar." But Luke 2:1-2 is not meant to be that exact.

A popular argument in defense of Luke 2:2 is that Quirinius was made the governor of Syria twice, citing certain though scant historical evidence to back up this claim. It might be true, but the argument is unnecessary. Such a claim does more to defend Josephus's flawed dates than it does to clear Luke of any possible discrepancies.

The gospel of Luke provides a historical and eyewitness account (Luke 1:1-2). His information and attention to detail are impeccable. Josephus was born after Jesus' death, resurrection, and ascension into heaven. It's foolish to insist we take Josephus' word over Luke's. Josephus has been shown to be wrong on numerous occasions, but the Bible is proven true time and time again, fulfilling the very claim that Scripture has made about itself: "Every word of God proves true" (Proverbs 30:5).

The author of the Bible is not merely the men who wrote it, "but men spoke from God as they were carried along by the Holy Spirit" (2 Peter 1:21). We should certainly test all things, for the Bible instructs us to. But it would do well for us to take the word of God over the word of any man. His is the word that leads to everlasting life.

REFLECTION

In Acts 17:26, we read that God "made from one man every nation of mankind to live on all the face of the earth, having determined allotted periods and the boundaries of their dwelling place." Do you know the story of how your mother and father met? What circumstances brought your parents together which then led to your birth? How does this make you appreciate how God has worked all things according to the counsel of His will? If you're reading this book as a family, sing together the hymn *O Little Town of Bethlehem*. Here are the lyrics:[16]

> *O Little town of Bethlehem,*
> *How still we see thee lie!*
> *Above thy deep and dreamless sleep*
> *The silent stars go by;*
> *Yet in thy dark streets shineth*
> *The everlasting Light;*
> *The hopes and fears of all the years*
> *Are met in thee tonight.*

---

[16] Brooks, Phillips. "O Little Town of Bethlehem" *(Hymns of Grace)*. Hymn 242.

For Christ is born of Mary,
And gathered all above,
While mortals sleep, the angels keep
Their watch of wondering love.
O morning stars, together
Proclaim the holy birth,
And praises sing to God the King,
And peace to men on earth!

How silently, how silently
The wondrous gift is given!
So God imparts to human hearts
The blessings of His heaven.
No ear may hear His coming,
But in this world of sin,
Where meek souls will receive Him, still
The dear Christ enters in.

O holy child of Bethlehem!
Descend to us, we pray;
Cast out our sin, and enter in,
Be born in us today!
We hear the Christmas angels
The great glad tidings tell;
O come to us, abide with us,
Our Lord, Immanuel!

Myth #4

Mary and Joseph were turned away by an innkeeper.

Picture this—A young couple just traveled a hundred miles to arrive at their destination in the middle of the night. The wife is clearly pregnant. She could give birth any minute. Her frantic husband knocks on the door of the local inn, and an old man, the innkeeper, opens the door a crack.

"What do you want?" the innkeeper huffs.

"Please, sir," the husband replies. "My wife is about to give birth—tonight, even. We need a room right away!"

The innkeeper's eyes widen. "At this time of night?" he exclaims. "Have you not heard there is a census going on? I've got people here from all over. There are no rooms left!"

"Nothing at all?" the husband says.

"I'm sorry," the innkeeper mutters. He starts to close the door, but the husband puts his hand out and stops him.

"Please!" the husband begs. "We're desperate. I'll take anything — anything you have!"

The innkeeper rubs his beard. He felt sorry for the young man and his pregnant wife. But what could he do? Still, he couldn't turn away a pregnant woman to have her baby in the middle of the town square. Finally, he comes up with a solution. "Well, there's the barn in the back. You'd have to share it with the animals. It's not the best, but it's all I've got."

"We'll take it," the husband says.

He escorts his wife on their donkey to the rear of the inn where there's a stable, full of donkeys, cows, sheep, and goats. The husband makes a comfortable place for his bride in a bed of hay. He apologizes about it not being the Hilton. Lovingly, she says it's wonderful.

That night she gives birth to her firstborn son. They wrap him in swaddling cloths and lay him in the animal's feed trough, because there was no room for them in the inn. No one was willing to give them a place to stay. No one realized that they had just turned away the Savior of the world.

What I've just described to you is the Christmas story, right?

Nope. It's a figment of our imaginations. That's not how the birth of Christ took place.

In Luke 2:7 we read, "And she gave birth to her firstborn son and wrapped Him in swaddling cloths and laid Him in a manger, because there was no place for them in the inn." This *one verse* taken out of context has led to three common Christmas myths: Mary and Joseph arrived in Bethlehem at the last minute, they were turned away by an innkeeper, so Mary gave birth to the Savior of the world in a barn. None of that is accurate.

It was because of the census decree that Joseph brought his pregnant wife, Mary, from Nazareth to Bethlehem to be registered. The picture we're often given is that they traveled alone with Mary on the back of a donkey. They could also have journeyed by horse, camel, or on a wagon pulled by draft animals like oxen. However they went, it is unlikely that they traveled alone.

As said in the previous chapter, this registration was a family affair, and Joseph and Mary may have traveled with other members of their tribe. The journey from Nazareth to Bethlehem was about 100 miles (150 km), which they would have tried to cover in a week between two Sabbaths. In Luke 2:44, we are told the family traveled as part of a group when they left Jerusalem after the Passover. Their trip to Bethlehem may have been in similar company.

Traveling alone was not safe. In Luke 10, Jesus told His famous parable about the good Samaritan. At the start of the parable, He said, "A man was going down from Jerusalem to Jericho, and he fell among robbers, who stripped him and beat him and departed, leaving him half-dead." Lone travelers had to be aware of that kind of danger. Of course, the Lord protected Joseph and Mary wherever they went, but it is still more likely that they journeyed among others, if even a small group.

Upon arriving in Bethlehem, Mary was not in the throes of labor pains. Luke 2:6 says, "And while they were there, the time came for her to give birth." So they had been in Bethlehem a while. Joseph would not have dragged his wife from Nazareth nine months pregnant, risking that she could have gone into labor while they were *en route.*

But that still doesn't explain why Luke 2:7 says that Mary wrapped her baby in swaddling cloths and laid Him in a manger "because there was no room for them *in the inn."* If they lived in a residence, why was Jesus put in an animal's feed trough? And why did Luke mention an inn? I'll talk about the manger in the next chapter, but for now let's focus on this word "inn."

We might think of an inn as being like a motel, but the word *inn* can describe any place of lodging that is not one's own home. Keep in mind that the New Testament was written in Greek only later to be translated into English. The Greek word for inn is κατάλυμα *(kataluma),* and it's commonly translated "guest room." The word comes up again in Luke 22:11 to describe the upper room where Jesus and His disciples had their last supper.

There were no commercial inns in first century Bethlehem. Misunderstanding the word "inn" has led many to insert another character in the Christmas story, one that Luke doesn't mention—an innkeeper. Every Christmas, there are preachers who deliver entire sermons about this nonexistent figure. Some pastors have even dressed the part and given a first-person account of the Christmas story from the perspective of the innkeeper. The moral of the story is often that we have a Christian duty to help those in need, and if we don't, we could very well be rejecting the Savior Himself—just like the innkeeper did on that first Christmas night.

Doing this is certainly not heresy, but there are better ways to tell others, "Love your neighbor," without adding to the Bible or turning the gospel into a tale of moralism. The Christmas story is not a story about how we need to help those in need. We are the ones in need, and Jesus is our help.

The Bible says all have sinned and fallen short of the glory of God, and the wages of sin is death. But the free gift of God is eternal life through Jesus Christ our Lord (Romans 3:23, 6:23). God sent His Son from heaven to this earth, where He lived the perfect life we could not live, and died the death we were supposed to die, taking the wrath of God upon Himself for our sins. All who believe in Him will not perish, but we will have everlasting life.

One of my favorite Christmas carols is *O Come, O*

Come Emmanuel, translated to English from the Latin hymn *Veni, Veni, Emmanuel*. There's a verse that goes like this:

> *O Come, Thou Rod of Jesse, free*
> *Thine own from Satan's tyranny.*
> *From depths of Hell, Thy people save,*
> *And give them victory o'er the grave.*
> *Rejoice! Rejoice! Emmanuel*
> *Shall come to thee, O Israel.*[17]

True Israel are the followers of Jesus, who has saved His people from the depths of hell and given victory over the grave to everyone who believes in Him. We're the ones in need. Jesus is our Savior. That's the story of Christmas.

REFLECTION
Sing the hymn *O Come, O Come Emmanuel* together. Here are the lyrics:

> *O Come, O come, Emmanuel,*
> *And ransom captive Israel*
> *That mourns in lonely exile here*
> *Until the Son of God appear*
> *Rejoice! Rejoice! Emmanuel*
> *Shall come to thee, O Israel!*

---

[17] Traditional. "O Come, O Come Emmanuel" *(Hymns of Grace)*. Hymn 218.

O come, Thou Dayspring, come and cheer
Our spirits by Thine advent here;
Disperse the gloomy clouds of night,
And death's dark shadows put to flight.
Rejoice! Rejoice! Emmanuel
Shall come to thee, O Israel!

O come, Thou Rod of Jesse, free
Thine own from Satan's tyranny;
From depths of hell Thy people save,
And give them victory o'er the grave.
Rejoice! Rejoice! Emmanuel
Shall come to thee, O Israel!

O come, Desire of nations, bind
All peoples in one heart and mind.
Bid envy, strife, and quarrels cease;
Fill the whole world with heaven's peace.
Rejoice! Rejoice! Emmanuel
Shall come to thee, O Israel!

How has Jesus saved you from Satan's tyranny? How do you know that you have victory over the grave by faith in Him? If you are not yet a Christian, who can you talk to about it?

Myth #5

Jesus was born in a barn.

Whether acted out by children in church, cast in small figurines in a home, or set up as a life-sized spectacle on the front lawn, the nativity scene has become a Christmas stable—I'm sorry, *staple*.

The word "nativity" comes from the Latin word *nativitas,* meaning "arisen by birth." Legend has it that a thirteenth century friar known as St. Francis of Assisi introduced the first nativity scene, which he set up with living animals and an empty manger as a visual while he preached the gospel.[18]

Your traditional nativity contains figurines of Mary and Joseph kneeling beside baby Jesus in a manger. You may also have a couple of shepherds with expressions of wonder on their faces. Present with the shepherds are their sheep, and there might be other animals like cows or a donkey. Don't forget the three kings with their gifts of gold, frankincense,

---

[18] Anthony, Gerard-Marie. *The Deacon: Icon of Christ, Icon of Hope* (Gerard-Marie Anthony, 2015). Pg. 77-78.

and myrrh. You might also add an angel standing nearby or suspended over the scene.

All of this is set under a cut-away stable with grass and hay inside. After all, as everyone knows, Jesus was born in a barn, right?

Not true.

Contrary to popular belief, Jesus was not born in a stable. This myth has come about partly because we live in a different time and culture, but mostly it's because the Scripture has been misinterpreted. That error has been repeated over and over for so long, we think that's how the story goes. But just as the gospel of Luke never mentions an innkeeper, there's no stable in the Christmas story either.

Returning again to Luke 2:6-7, we read, "And while they were there, the time came for her to give birth. And she gave birth to her firstborn son and wrapped Him in swaddling cloths and laid Him in a manger, because there was no place for them in the inn."

It's this word "manger" (from the Greek word *phatne*) that has led many to conclude the setting of the birth of Christ was in a stable, or a structure in which livestock are kept. A manger is an animal's feed trough—hence why we also depict the birth of Christ surrounded by sheep, cattle, and donkeys. The word is used again in Luke 2:12 when the angels told shepherds they would find the Savior "wrapped in swaddling cloths and lying in a manger."

So if baby Jesus was placed in a manger, why is it unreasonable to assume he was born in a barn? Because we're imagining with western world minds in the twenty-first century rather than thinking of a first-century setting in the Middle East.

The common dwelling in first-century Palestine [19] was comprised of two levels—the upper room was for dining and sleeping, the lower level for work and fellowship. At night, the animals would be brought into the home to ensure that they wouldn't run away or be stolen. Obviously, the animals remained on the lower level while the occupants stayed upstairs. The heat generated by the animals also helped to keep the home warm.

Remember that Joseph and Mary had been in Bethlehem for at least several weeks by the time Jesus was born. They didn't arrive with Mary in the throes of labor-pains. Because they returned to the place of their lineage, they would have been staying with family. The house was full of people who had returned to register for the census.

The upper room or "inn" of the house was occupied. Therefore, Jesus was born downstairs, and a manger was made His crib. Mary likely preferred to give birth downstairs instead of being surrounded by a bunch of people! It certainly would have been more private.

---

[19] Palestine here is in reference to the historic region, not the modern state.

Now, just because Jesus was born in the place where animals are kept, that doesn't mean animals were present. Joseph and Mary weren't staying with a bunch of heartless aunts and uncles who told her to grin and bear it, forcing her to give birth under the rear end of a cow. The animals would have stayed outside.

Keep in mind that Luke is giving an account of a great historical event, and all of these elements are important to the story. The baby Jesus was wrapped in swaddling cloths and laid in a manger because there was no room upstairs. These are not just standalone facts. It was customary to wrap newborn babies in swaddling cloths, but it wasn't customary to lay them in mangers. Why did Mary put him there? Because "there was no room for them" in the upper room of the house where everyone slept. A lot of people were in this house.

This is significant for what Luke intended to convey. In Luke 1:2, he introduced his gospel by saying that this was an account of "eyewitnesses." So here in Luke 2:6-7, he's showing the reader that there were *many witnesses* to the birth of Christ! Mary and Joseph weren't by themselves out in a barn. "There was no place for them in the inn" means the house they were in was full of family!

A second thing to consider is that Luke is setting up the next part of the story where he introduces another group of witnesses—*shepherds,* to whom angels announced that the Messiah had come. Here is the angel's message again with the last part in italics for emphasis:

> And the angel said to them, "Fear not, for behold I bring you good news of great joy that will be for all the people. For unto you is born this day in the city of David a Savior, who is Christ the Lord. And this will be a sign for you: *you will find a baby wrapped in swaddling cloths and lying in a manger.*"

It was necessary for Luke to say in his narrative that Jesus was wrapped in swaddling cloths and placed in a manger because it was part of the angel's announcement to the shepherds.

The *sign* of Jesus' birth is understood in two ways. First, the angels announced that the birth of Jesus was the fulfillment of the "sign" that God promised through the prophet Isaiah: "Therefore the Lord Himself will give you a sign. Behold the virgin shall conceive and bear a son and shall call His name Immanuel" (Isaiah 7:14). The angels said that this baby born in Bethlehem was the Messiah who had been foretold.

The second way this sign is understood is in how the shepherds would find the Christ-child: wrapped in swaddling cloths and lying in a manger. *Wrapped in swaddling cloths* indicated to the shepherds that this miracle-baby was a newborn. Bethlehem was a small town with no more than a few hundred people. Still, there may have been a few babies. The shepherds were looking for the baby who had just been born.

In a manger told the shepherds where the baby was. The angel didn't exactly set the shepherds up with a street-address, but "in a manger" was enough. Since animals were outside during the day and inside at night, their feed troughs were likely built into the wall, half-outside and half-inside. This meant the shepherds could find the baby without knocking on doors or tromping through someone's home.

The shepherds found the baby just as the angel had said: wrapped in swaddling cloths and lying in a manger—having been born in a home, not in a barn.

If this ruins your perspective of Jesus' lowly beginnings, it shouldn't. Instead of being born in the palace, which was visible from Bethlehem, the King of kings was born in a peasant's home, in the part where the animals sleep.

We read in 2 Corinthians 8:9, "For you know the grace of our Lord Jesus Christ, that though He was rich, yet for your sake He became poor, so that you by His poverty might become rich." Jesus Christ left His throne in heaven, took on human flesh, and became obedient to the point of death, even death on a cross. He became nothing so that through Him, we might have everything!

Therefore, we should be imitators of Christ our

Savior: "Do nothing from selfish ambition or conceit, but in humility count others more significant than yourselves. Let each of you look not only to his own interests, but also the interests of others. Have this mind among yourselves, which is yours in Christ Jesus" (Philippians 2:3-5).

REFLECTION

Continue reading Philippians 2 and look at verses 6-11. One of the ways, if not the greatest of ways, that we are to consider the needs of others is by sharing the gospel with them. Those who are not Christians still need to hear the good news: "that Christ died for our sins in accordance with the Scriptures, that He was buried, that He was raised on the third day in accordance with the Scriptures" (1 Corinthians 15:3-4). Those who believe in Jesus will be saved! Sing the following hymn together, *Go, Tell It on the Mountain.* Here are the lyrics:[20]

> *Go, tell it on the mountain,*
> *Over the hills and everywhere;*
> *Go, tell it on the mountain*
> *That Jesus Christ is born!*
>
> *While shepherds kept their watching*
> *O'er silent flocks by night,*

---

[20] Work, John W. "Go, Tell It on the Mountain" *(Hymns of Grace).* Hymn 225.

Behold throughout the heavens
There shone a holy light.
(chorus)

The shepherds feared and trembled
When lo! above the earth
Rang out the angel chorus
That hailed our Savior's birth.
(chorus)

Down in a lowly manger
The humble Christ was born,
And God sent us salvation
That blessed Christmas morn.
(chorus)

Myth #6
Angels sang to shepherds.

One of the most famous Christmas carols is *Hark! The Herald Angels Sing*, written in 1739 by Charles Wesley, later to be fitted to a musical piece written separately by Felix Mendelssohn over a century later. The popularity of this hymn is largely the reason why we assume angels sang to shepherds on that first Christmas night. After all, it's right there in the title: *Hark! The Herald Angels Sing!*

This is mentioned in many carols. In *O Come All Ye Faithful*, one of the verses begins, "Sing choirs of angels, sing in exultation!"[21] In the first verse of the hymn *It Came Upon a Midnight Clear*, we sing:

> *The world in solemn stillness lay*
> *To hear the angels sing.* [22]

---

[21] Wade, John Francis. "O Come All Ye Faithful" *(Hymns of Grace)*. Hymn 231.
[22] Sears, Edmund H. "It Came Upon a Midnight Clear" *(Hymns of Grace)*. Hymn 246.

However, the Bible doesn't say that angels sang. In fact, *no where* in the Bible are angels depicted as singing ever—not on earth, nor in revelations of the future, nor in visions of heaven.

Now, this is a particularly minor point. If you want to imagine angels singing to shepherds, that's fine. But marvel with me as we consider that God has given certain gifts and privileges to people—made in His image—that He has not given even to His holy angels. Looking again at Luke 2:8-14, we read:

> And in the same region there were shepherds out in the field, keeping watch over their flock by night. And an angel of the Lord appeared to them, and the glory of the Lord shone around them, and they were filled with great fear.
>
> And the angel said to them, "Fear not, for behold, I bring you good news of great joy that will be for all the people. For unto you is born this day in the city of David a Savior, who is Christ the Lord. And this will be a sign for you: you will find a baby wrapped in swaddling cloths and lying in a manger."
>
> And suddenly there was with the angel a multitude of the heavenly host praising God and saying, "Glory to God in the highest! And on earth peace among those with whom He is pleased!"

Notice that the text says "a multitude of the heavenly host" was "praising God and *saying*," not singing. The Greek word is λέγω *(lego)*, which means "to say." The word is used again in Luke 21:5 where we read about some people who *"were speaking* of the temple."

Isaiah 44:23 says, "Sing, O heavens, for the Lord has done it." Who else could sing from heaven but the angels, right? But when you look at the context, you see Isaiah was being figurative by personifying creation. Going on, we read, "Shout O depths of the earth; break forth into singing, O mountains, O forest, and every tree in it!" In Isaiah 49:13, we read, "Sing for joy, O heavens, and exult, O earth; break forth, O mountains into singing!"

Job 38:7 says, "The morning stars sang together, and all the sons of God shouted for joy." But this is amidst very figurative language where God also says that He laid the foundation of the earth. Does the earth sit on a foundation? Of course not. Elsewhere in Job we are told He "hangs the earth on nothing" (Job 26:7).

In Jeremiah 51:48, we read, "Then the heavens and the earth, and all that is in them, shall sing for joy over Babylon, for the destroyers shall come against them out of the north, declares the Lord." That might be the closest we get to a picture of angels singing. But as with Isaiah and Job, the language in this portion of Jeremiah is poetic and figurative.

In the last book of the Bible, we read about singing in heaven. Revelation 14:2-3 says, "And I heard a voice from heaven like the roar of many waters and like the sound of loud thunder. The voice I heard was like the sound of harpists playing on their harps, and they were singing a new song before the throne and before the four living creatures and before the elders. No one could learn that song except [the ones] who had been redeemed from the earth."

In the next chapter, John sees a multitude holding harps in their hands. "And they sing the song of Moses, the servant of God, and the song of the Lamb, saying, 'Great and amazing are your deeds, O Lord God the Almighty! Just and true are your ways, O King of the nations!'" (Revelation 15:3).

Music and song appear to be a gift that God has given exclusively to mankind to use for His glory. When God rescued the Israelites by drowning the Egyptians in the Red Sea, the people sang, "I will sing to the Lord, for He has triumphed gloriously; the horse and his rider He has thrown into the sea" (Exodus 15:1). Miriam, Moses's sister, led the women in singing (v.20-21).

King David wrote many songs of praise unto God which make up the Psalms. Psalm 89:1 says, "I will sing of the steadfast love of the Lord, forever; with my mouth I will make known your faithfulness to all generations." Psalm 101:1 says, "I will sing of steadfast love and justice; to you, O Lord, I will make music." Psalm 108:1 says, "My heart is steadfast, O God! I will sing and make melody with all of my being!"

The songs David wrote were not just happy tunes. Even in times of grief and lament, David still sang unto God: "How long must I take counsel in my soul and have sorrow in my heart all the day? How long shall my enemy be exalted over me? But I have trusted in your steadfast love; my heart shall rejoice in your salvation. I will sing to the Lord, because He has dealt bountifully with me" (Psalm 13:2, 5-6).

This is not merely a privilege—singing to God is commanded! "Sing to God, sing praises to His name; lift up a song to Him who rides through the deserts; His name is the Lord; exult before Him" (Psalm 68:4). "Oh sing to the Lord a new song; sing to the Lord, all the earth. Sing to the Lord, bless His name; tell of His salvation from day to day" (Psalm 96:1-2). "Serve the Lord with gladness! Come into His presence with singing" (Psalm 100:2).

The church is also called to sing together, lifting praises unto God through music. Ephesians 5:18-19 says to us, "Be filled with the Spirit, addressing one another in psalms and hymns and spiritual songs, singing and making melody to the Lord with your heart." We read in Colossians 3:16, "Let the word of Christ dwell in you richly, teaching and admonishing one another in all wisdom, singing psalms and hymns and spiritual songs, with thankfulness in your hearts to God."

Who knows if angels sing? But we know that God has given people the gift of song, and we are to praise Him with music. The Lord has bestowed blessings upon His people even holy angels have not received—namely salvation. God has no plan to redeem the angels. Those angels that are fallen, that were cast from heaven with Satan (Revelation 12:4), have no chance to be restored to their former dwelling place. They will perish on the day of judgment in eternal fire, along with those who did not follow Christ (Matthew 25:41).

Jesus died not redeem angels but to purify a people for His own possession (Titus 2:14). It is by the grace of God that we are saved from His judgment by the perfect sacrifice of Christ, for all those who believe in Him. In 1 Peter 1:10-12, the Apostle Peter wrote the following:

> Concerning this salvation, the prophets who prophesied about the grace that was to be yours searched and inquired carefully, inquiring what person or time the Spirit of Christ in them was indicating when He predicted the sufferings of Christ and subsequent glories. It was revealed to them that they were serving not themselves but you, in the things that have now been announced to you through those who preached the good

news to you by the Holy Spirit sent from heaven, things into which angels long to look.

Though the angels enter in and out of the very presence of God, these heavenly hosts do not get to experience the redemptive grace of God. That is a privilege God has given only to His elect. We are "justified by His grace as a gift, through the redemption that is in Christ Jesus, whom God put forward as a propitiation by His blood, to be received by faith" (Romans 3:24-25).

The promise of this coming grace was fulfilled on that first Christmas night in Bethlehem over 2,000 years ago. Angels delivered the good news to shepherds, and they praised the Lord in their presence: "Glory to God in the highest! And on earth peace among those with whom He is pleased!"

A message spoken *by* angels *for* mankind. That's worth singing about!

REFLECTION

Sing together *Hark! The Herald Angels Sing*.[23] Yes, I just argued that the angels probably didn't sing to shepherds, but again, it is a minor point, and this is still a great song, containing the gospel in its lyrics. Here they are to help you:

---

[23] Wesley, Charles. "Hark! The Herald Angels Sing" *(Hymns of Grace)*. Hymn 238.

Hark! the herald angels sing,
"Glory to the newborn King;
Peace on earth, and mercy mild,
God and sinners reconciled!"
Joyful, all ye nations rise,
Join the triumph of the skies;
With angelic hosts proclaim,
"Christ is born in Bethlehem!"
Hark! the herald angels sing,
"Glory to the newborn King!"

Christ, by highest heaven adored;
Christ, the everlasting Lord!
Late in time behold Him come,
Offspring of the Virgin's womb:
Veiled in flesh the Godhead see;
Hail incarnate Deity,
Pleased as man with men to dwell,
Jesus, our Emmanuel.
Hark! the herald angels sing,
"Glory to the newborn King!"

Hail, the heaven-born Prince of Peace!
Hail, the Son of Righteousness!
Light and life to all He brings,
Risen with healing in His wings.
Mild He lays His glory by,
Born that man no more may die,
Born to raise the sons of earth,
Born to give them second birth.

Hark! the herald angels sing,
"Glory to the newborn King!"

What are some of your favorite songs to sing? How do these songs give glory to God? Do you sing praises to God in church? How do you think you could incorporate a time of singing in your personal time with God? Or during family time?

Myth #7
Three kings attended the birth of Jesus.

In Matthew chapter 26, Jesus was arrested by the chief priests and the pharisees and found guilty for speaking blasphemy — He had proclaimed Himself to be the Messiah, the Son of God. The pharisees wanted to put Jesus to death, but they could not do that without permission from the Romans. So Jesus was brought before Pontius Pilate, Roman governor of the province of Judea.

According to Matthew 27:11, when Jesus stood before the governor, Pilate asked Him, "Are you the King of the Jews?" Jesus said, "You have said so." The chief priests and the elders continued to hurl accusations at Him in the presence of Pilate, but Jesus said nothing to their charges. Pilate said to Him, "'Do you not hear how many things they testify against you?' But He gave him no answer, not even to a single charge, so that the governor was greatly amazed" (Matthew 27:11-14).

The story of Jesus' crucifixion is typically part of the Easter story. But this is a Christmas book, not an

Easter book, so surely you know I'm about to tie this back into the Christmas story. Let's go back to the start of Matthew, when a group of foreigners came to Jerusalem looking for the King of the Jews.

Matthew 2:1-2 says, "Now after Jesus was born in Bethlehem of Judea in the days of Herod the king, behold, wise men from the east came to Jerusalem, saying, 'Where is He who has been born king of the Jews? For we saw His star when it rose and have come to worship Him.'"

These *wise men* have been imagined in many ways, but the traditional depiction is as three kings. This is the version you see in most nativity sets, plays, and films. The magi visiting the Christ-child has been illustrated in many classic paintings, some hundreds of years old. But perhaps no one man is more responsible for the picture of *three kings* than an Episcopal priest named John Henry Hopkins, Jr.

In 1857, Hopkins wrote his famous carol *We Three Kings of Orient Are*. Hopkins arranged the song to be sung by three male voices. The three men sing the first verse and the chorus in three-part harmony. The next three verses are sung as solos with each vocalist playing a different "king"—the first one bringing gold, the second frankincense, and the third myrrh.

It's a beautiful hymn—not only in its composition but also the theology in its lyrics. The baby Jesus was presented with gold because He is a king—the King of kings, who is "over us all to reign."[24] He received frankincense for Christ became a fragrant offering unto God. And the gift of myrrh, used in Jesus' death and burial (see Mark 15:23 and John 19:39), is meant to foreshadow of the death of Christ as a sacrifice for our sins.

It's obvious where Hopkins got the idea to limit his wise men to *three*—Matthew says that the magi brought three gifts, so Hopkins wrote his song for three characters. But where Hopkins got the idea to call them "kings" is not as clear. Maybe he was taking creative liberties to fit the rhythm of the song, or perhaps his reasoning was more Scriptural. After all, Psalm 72:10-11 prophesied of Jesus:

> May the kings of Tarshish and of the coastlands
>   render him tribute;
> may the kings of Sheba and Seba
>   bring gifts!
> May all kings fall down before him,
>   all nations serve him!

A thousand years after that Psalm was written, kings officials from the east came and brought gifts to the King of kings, and Matthew 2:11 says that they "fell down and worshiped Him." It would seem then that the magi are in fulfillment of Psalm 72, where they are referred to, however informally, as "kings."

---

[24] Hopkins Jr., John Henry. "We Three Kings of Orient Are" *(Hymns of Grace).* Hymn 228.

We are certain though that more than just three men came from the east to worship the Christ-child. "Wise men" in the Greek is the word *magoi*, or magi, from which we get words like magic or magician. Magi were priests of Zoroastrianism, the state religion of the Medes and Persians beginning in the 6th century B.C. These priests practiced a variety of what we might refer to as "magic arts," including soothsaying, divination, astrology, and interpreting dreams. They were also appointed for their wisdom, political council, and knowledge of history.[25]

Right at the start of the 6th century B.C., God exiled Israel into the hands of their enemies because of their unrepentant sin. They were first exiled to the Babylonians and later to the Medes and Persians. Yet God showed favor to a Hebrew named Daniel, who became a trusted wiseman appointed to the courts of kings like Nebuchadnezzar II of Babylon and Darius the Mede of Persia. The Bible says, "Daniel became distinguished above all the other high officials and satraps, because an excellent spirit was in him" (Daniel 6:3).

The wise men Daniel oversaw would have included magi, and they became very acquainted with Hebrew prophesy. Daniel himself saw a vision of a great King, "like a son of man" (Daniel 7:13-14):

---

[25] Tenney, Merrill C. *The Zondervan Pictorial Encyclopedia of the Bible* (Zondervan, Grand Rapids, MI; 1975). Vol. 4, Pg. 31-34.

And to Him was given dominion
and glory and a kingdom,
that all peoples, nations, and languages
should serve Him.
His dominion is an everlasting dominion,
which shall not pass away,
and His kingdom one
that shall not be destroyed.

Over five hundred years later, when Magi came riding into Jerusalem saying, "Where is He who has been born King of the Jews?" they knew whom they were looking for because they knew the Scriptures. Matthew 2:3 says, "When Herod the king heard this, he was troubled, and all Jerusalem with him." The magi's caravan was large enough to attract a lot of attention, so again, it's evident there were more than three of them.

Since the writings the magi read were Hebrew, they figured any Jew in their capital city would know where to find the Christ child. But Israel was so far from God, King Herod had to consult his own wise men to know what the magi were asking about. Where was the Christ to be born, he asked them? "In Bethlehem of Judea," the scribes said, "for so it was written by the prophet: 'And you, O Bethlehem, in the land of Judah, are by no means least among the rulers of Judah; for from you shall come a ruler who will shepherd my people Israel'" (Matthew 2:5-6).

Israel was in such a spiritual famine that the people did not even know their own Scriptures, the word of God given to them through His prophets. Foreign priests from a distant land came looking for the Messiah, but the Jews should have been the ones looking for Him. Every resident of Jerusalem and in fact all of Judea should have been able to say, "Yes! Our Messiah is born in Bethlehem! Come and see!" But their foolish hearts were darkened.

Herod summoned the magi to him and was able to ascertain when the star had appeared. He told them they would find what they were looking for in Bethlehem. "Go and search diligently for the child," he said. "And when you have found him, bring me word, that I too may come and worship him."

The magi followed the star just a few more miles to the south until it stopped over a house in Bethlehem. The text says, "They rejoiced exceedingly with great joy," and when they went inside and found the Christ child with Mary His mother, they fell down and worshiped Him. Then they opened to Him their gifts — treasures of gold, frankincense, and myrrh."

These were regal gifts — offerings you would give to a king. When dignitaries came from a far-off land, they would bring gold and spices to the monarch. In 1 Kings 10:10, the Queen of Sheba brought King Solomon "gold and a very great quantity of spices."

In other words, she brought him gold, frankincense, and myrrh. Don't gloss over the significance of these gifts. The magi understood Jesus to be a king according to the prophecies made about Him. The rest of Israel did not understand.

John 1:11-13 says, "He came to His own, and His own people did not receive Him. But to all who did receive Him, who believed in His name, He gave the right to become children of God, who were born, not of blood nor of the will of the flesh nor of the will of man, but of God."

Now remember, there were no commercial inns in Bethlehem and no innkeepers to turn them away. Where did this traveling group of magi stay? They would have stayed in tents just outside the city limits of Bethlehem. Matthew 2:12 says, "Being warned in a dream not to return to Herod, they departed to their own country by another way." The text doesn't tell us how soon after arriving in Bethlehem that this dream was given to them, but likely their stay was very short.

Herod was enraged when the wise men didn't return, "and he sent and killed all the male children in Bethlehem and in all that region who were two years old or under, according to the time that he had ascertained from the wise men" (v.16).

From this part of the story we know the wise men didn't arrive at the time of Jesus' birth. The journey from Persia would have taken several months if not a couple of seasons. They knew Jesus had already been born for that was the question they came asking: "Where is He *who has been born?*" Jesus may have been anywhere from six to eighteen months old at the time of the magi's arrival. Herod ordered the murder of every male child "two years old or under," just to cover his bases.

Like the Magi, Joseph was also warned of Herod in a dream. He took Mary and Jesus in the middle of the night and fled to Egypt. There they remained until Herod died of a serious illness a short time later. That was quite a drama, and all because a caravan of foreigners came asking, "Where is He who has been born king of the Jews?" Children were even murdered because of it.

Now fast forward over thirty years later to Jesus standing before Pontius Pilate. When Pilate asked Him, "Are you the King of the Jews?" in the context of Matthew's gospel, what he was essentially saying to Jesus was this: *"So you're the one who has stirred up all this commotion, starting with those wise men years ago and all the way up until now."*

When Jesus was crucified, Pilate had a sign hung over Him which read, "This is Jesus, the King of the Jews." It was written in Aramaic, Latin, and Greek. When the chief priests saw it, they said to Pilate, "Do not write, 'The King of the Jews,' but rather, 'This man said, I am King of the Jews.'" Pilate replied, "What I have written, I have written."

Even Pilate understood, connecting all the pieces together, that this Jesus was more than an ordinary man. However, it is unlikely that he ever believed Jesus was truly the King of kings. According to Eusebius of Caesarea, Pilate killed himself just a few years after Jesus' death and resurrection.[26] Both Herod and Pilate tried to destroy Jesus, but Herod and Pilate were destroyed instead.

Daniel 2:21 says, "He changes times and seasons; He removes kings and sets up kings; He gives wisdom to the wise and knowledge to those who have understanding."

This is Jesus, the King to whom all other kings and wise men bow.

REFLECTION

What is your favorite gift you received at Christmas? What made that gift special? What is it that makes a gift most special to you — the value of the gift, or the thought that went into the gift? How valuable is the gift of God's Son? Sing the following hymn *We Three Kings of Orient Are.* If there are enough in your group, maybe you could split up and have a different person sing a different part! Then everyone sing the chorus together. Here are the lyrics:

We three kings of Orient are:
Bearing gifts we traverse afar

---

[26] Eusebius, *Ecclesiastical History.* 2.7.

Field and fountain, moor and mountain
Following yonder star

Chorus:
Oh, star of wonder, star of night,
Star with royal beauty bright,
Westward leading, still proceeding,
Guide us to thy perfect light.

Born a King on Bethlehem's plain:
Gold I bring to crown Him again,
King forever, ceasing never,
Over us all to reign.

Frankincense to offer have I,
Incense owns a Deity nigh;
Prayer and praising, all men raising,
Worship Him, God on high.

Myrrh is mine, its bitter perfume
Breathes a life of gathering gloom.
Sorrowing, sighing, bleeding, dying,
Sealed in the stone-cold tomb.

Glorious now behold Him arise:
King and God and Sacrifice;
Alleluia, Alleluia!
Earth to heaven replies.

Myth #8

The star of Bethlehem was a natural phenomenon.

Again, we read in Matthew 2:1-2, "Now after Jesus was born in Bethlehem of Judea in the days of Herod the king, behold, wise men from the east came to Jerusalem, saying, 'Where is He who has been born king of the Jews? For we saw His star when it rose and have come to worship Him.'"

Much speculation has been made about this star the wise men followed. In more recent decades, theologians and scientists, skeptics and conspiracy theorists have combed history looking for mentions of major astronomical phenomena that might explain the star of Bethlehem.

Back in the 1970s, a fellow by the name of David Hughes (no relation) claimed to have the answer. It really wasn't a star at all, Hughes said. It was a conjunction of the planets Jupiter and Saturn.[27]

Hughes recognized that these wise men were magi, astronomers and astrologers from the region of

---

[27] Hughes, David W. "The Star of Bethlehem" (*Nature,* 264, December 9, 1976). Pg. 513-517.

Babylon. They studied the movements of stars and planets as a means of divining how celestial events affected human affairs. When a bright new star appeared in the night, caused by Jupiter and Saturn coming close to one another in the sky, it caught the magi's attention. This conjunction didn't happen just once—it happened three times over a short period from about 7 to 6 B.C.[28]

The magi believed this rare occurrence was an omen speaking a message, so they decided to follow the light to see where it led. Tim O'Brien, associate director of Jodrell Bank Observatory in Cheshire, England, told the *Bible Review*, "You would only get a triple conjunction like this about every 900 years. A triple conjunction of this kind ticks all the boxes."[29]

Another popular theory is that the light was a comet. Indeed, there just so happened to be a bright comet in the constellation of Capricorn recorded by Chinese astronomers in 5 B.C. But Hughes explained why the comet theory was unlikely.

"Quite a lot of people liked the comet idea, so it crops up in quite a lot of Christmas cards," Hughes said. "The snag is that they're not that rare. They were also commonly associated with the four D's—

[28] Parpola, Simo; "The Magi and the Star" (*Bible Review*, December, 2001). Pg. 16-23 and pg. 52-54.

[29] Gill, Victoria. *Star of Bethlehem: The astronomical explanations* (BBC, December 23, 2012). https://www.bbc.com/news/magazine-20730828

doom, death, disease, disaster. So if it did contain a message, it would have been a bad omen."[30]

Other theories about the star of Bethlehem have included the birth of a new star, the explosion of an old star, and the discovery of the planet Uranus. But none of these ideas are *bright* ideas (pun intended). A conjunction of planets is not that much brighter than other stars. In fact, I find it much more difficult to believe the star of Bethlehem was something natural rather than something supernatural.

After the magi met with King Herod and then continued to Bethlehem, the text says, "And behold, the star that they had seen when it rose went before them until it came to rest over the place where the child was. When they saw the star, they rejoiced exceedingly with great joy" (Matthew 2:9-10). So the star was always in the east *and it moved,* stopping over the house where Jesus was.

If God wanted to move heavenly bodies to guide foreign travelers to the Savior of the world, He could certainly do that. He's the Creator of heaven and earth—He can do what He wants! But if the star of Bethlehem really was an astral event way out in space, we would expect to find historical accounts from every part of the world marveling at such a sight. Yet all we have today, apart from Matthew's gospel, are a bunch of not-so-bright speculations.

One thing I believe Mr. Hughes got right is that

[30] Gill, BBC.

the star of Bethlehem was not actually a star. From the ground, it certainly looked like a star. But this bright light hung lower in the sky than the sun, moon, and stars as it guided the magi to the Savior.

A prophecy about a star that would appear at the time of Christ's birth was made in Numbers 24:16-17:

"The oracle of him who hears the words of God,
    and knows the knowledge of the Most High,
who sees the vision of the Almighty,
    falling down with his eyes uncovered:
I see Him, but not now;
    I behold Him, but not near:
a star shall come out of Jacob,
    and a scepter shall rise out of Israel;
it shall crush the forehead of Moab
    and break down all the sons of Sheth."

The magi read "not now" as meaning a distant time, and "not near" as a distant land. "Scepter" was a reference to a king. A "star" would rise out of "Jacob," who are the Jews, and "Israel" would be the place. All of this happened just as it was foretold!

The magi came to possess these sacred Scriptures when the Jews were exiled to the Babylonians six hundred years earlier. They knew whom they were looking for because they'd read about Him through the prophet Daniel.

The star itself remains a mystery. Was it just a

bright spot in thin air? Was it an angel? Was it visible in the day as well as at night? We assume the magi were night travelers, but Matthew doesn't tell us that. How do we know this star wasn't also visible by day? What if the magi found Jesus during the day and not at night? We'll never know for sure this side of heaven.

What we do know is that God used a star to lead men from Persia to find His Son. Jesus is a Savior given to the whole world, not just to the Jews. Even though He was born to the Jews as the prophets foretold, the Jews weren't looking for Him. Wise men from afar searched for Him, and when they found Him, they bowed down and worshiped Him.

Isaiah prophesied, "The people who walked in darkness have seen a great light; those who dwelt in a land of deep darkness, on them has light shone" (Isaiah 9:2).

In John 8:12, Jesus said, "I am the light of the world. Whoever follows me will not walk in darkness, but will have the light of life."

REFLECTION

Sing together the first couple of verses of the hymn *O Come All Ye Faithful.* One of these verses might not be as familiar to you, but it contains great truth about the Messiah. Here are the lyrics:[31]

---

[31] Wade, John F. "O Come Let Us Adore Him" *(Hymns of Grace).* Hymn 231.

O come, all ye faithful, joyful and triumphant
O come ye, O come ye to Bethlehem!
Come and behold Him, born the King of angels.
O come let us adore Him
O come let us adore Him
O come let us adore Him, Christ the Lord!

God of God, Light of Light eternal,
Lo, he abhors not the virgin's womb
Very God, begotten not created
O come let us adore Him
O come let us adore Him
O come let us adore Him, Christ the Lord!

What did Jesus mean when He said, "I am the light of the world," and "Whoever follows me will not walk in darkness"? In Matthew 5:14, Jesus said to His disciples, "You are the light of the world." If Jesus is the light of the world, what does it mean that we would also be lights in the world? (Hint: Look up Philippians 2:14-16.)

Myth #9
King Herod killed thousands of babies.

After the wise men had departed, an angel of the Lord appeared to Joseph in a dream and said, "Rise, take the child and His mother, and flee to Egypt, and remain there until I tell you, for King Herod is about to search for the child to destroy Him."

Matthew 2:14 says that they fled to Egypt during the night. On this journey, Joseph and Mary with their baby, Jesus, traveled alone—but of course we know they weren't really alone. One might wonder if the same star that guided the wise men to the Christ child also led Joseph and Mary to safety.

Some have argued this means the holy family were refugees (the statement is almost always made as part of a political argument). A refugee is someone forced to leave their country in order to escape war or persecution, or they have been displaced because of the devastating effects of a natural disaster. Joseph and Mary were certainly escaping from the wrath of Herod; however, they never left the Roman empire. It would have been more like moving from one state to another rather than fleeing an unstable territory as immigrants for a more stable yet foreign land.

Joseph and Mary went from Judea to Egypt using the gifts given to them by the magi to afford the journey and their stay. Where they stayed when they arrived in Egypt would have been within the large Jewish colony in Alexandria established centuries earlier.

After Joseph fled with Mary and Jesus, verse 16 says, "Then Herod, when he saw that he had been tricked by the wise men, became furious." Herod was a very insecure king, as is every ruler who does not believe that Jesus is King of kings and Lord of lords. If Jesus is King, then Herod isn't. If Jesus is Lord, then Caesar isn't. Their power and authority is limited. It's the same reason why governments today hate Christ, Christmas, or any public display of Christianity. It would mean acknowledging if not bowing to a higher authority.

These wise men from a distant land paid homage to another King, but they did not pay homage to Herod, and Herod considered this a betrayal. The only reason Herod went along with the wise men's mission in the first place was so they would come back and tell him where they found the baby. Herod intended to murder the child he believed was a threat to his throne.

Verse 16 goes on to say that in his anger, Herod "sent and killed all the male children in Bethlehem and in all that region who were two years old or under, according to the time that he had ascertained from the wise men." Then was fulfilled what was spoken by the prophet Jeremiah —

"A voice was heard in Ramah,
    weeping and loud lamentation,
Rachel weeping for her children;
    she refused to be comforted, because they are
    no more."

This is known to history as the massacre of the innocents, and it's scarcely accepted by academics as true. According to Lutheran minister and historian Paul L. Maier, "The massacre has been drenched with doubt by historians, biblical commentators, and biographers of Herod the Great. In fact, except for the Virgin Birth, no aspect of the Nativity has come under heavier critical challenge than the Infant Massacre at Bethlehem."[32]

Apart from this account in the book of Matthew, there are no other ancient historical references to the massacre ordered by Herod. Josephus does not mention it in his biography of Herod the Great in *Antiquities of the Jews*. One theory regarding the lack of evidence is that though Herod had ordered the

---

[32] Maier, Paul L., "Herod and the Infants of Bethlehem" (*Chronos Kairos Christos II*; edited by E. Jerry Vardaman; Mercer University Press, 1998). Pg. 169-170.

massacre, it was never carried out. However, this explanation would contradict Matthew who said that the slaughter of these children was prophesied in Jeremiah 31:15—a cry heard in Ramah, "Rachel weeping for her children."

Ramah was just a few miles to the north of Jerusalem, as far as Bethlehem was to the south. Ramah would have been in the vicinity of Herod's order. Rachel was the favorite wife of Jacob, and Jeremiah 31:15 is a reference to her offspring. Herod had no problem killing his own people as he'd also killed a wife, his brother-in-law, and three sons, as well as hundreds of others.[33]

The reason we're puzzled by the lack of extra-biblical evidence for the massacre is because the number of lives lost has been grossly overstated. And when I say "grossly overstated," I mean really, *really* overstated. The Byzantine liturgical calendar records that 14,000 "Holy Innocents" were slain by Herod at Bethlehem.[34] In the Coptic Orthodox Church, the "Doxology for the 144,000" is sung to remember 144,000 children killed by Herod.[35] A hundred and forty-four thousand is a crazy-high number that

---

[33] Tenney, Vol. 3, Pg. 136-138.

[34] Byzantine Catholic Church in America, 2019 Liturgical Calendar. http://www.byzcath.org/index.php/resources /calendars/2019-liturgical-calendar

[35] Doxology for the 144,000 Holy Infants (Holy Innocents). https://youtu.be/LCFyRoW4Apk

would have been about a quarter of the population of Jerusalem at that time.

Several renaissance artists have illustrated the *Massacre of the Innocents,* like Dutch painters Cornelis van Haarlem and Pieter Brueghel. Haarlem's scene is a depiction of a mass execution outside of a city with hundreds of lives lost, while Brueghel's version of the event happened in the middle of a town square with a band of foot soldiers carrying large spears. Italian painter Tintoretto also portrayed a public slaughter that looks like it happened in the streets of Jerusalem.

Outside of the Scriptures, the number of dead children and the size of the military campaign is believed to be so great that the story has become unbelievable. In reality, the number of lives lost was probably about twenty—a few in Bethlehem, and then another dozen or so in the surrounding towns. That's still a massacre. One mother losing one child at the hands of a tyrant would cause Rachel to weep in agony.

Keep in mind that Matthew 2:16 says, "Then Herod, when he saw that he had been tricked by the wise men, became furious, and he sent and killed *all the male children* in Bethlehem and in all that region who were two years old or under." These were only male children, not all infants. How many baby boys could there have been under the age of two in Bethlehem or any of the other small towns outside of

Jerusalem? The number of soldiers deployed to carry out the order would not have been high either.

But if Herod demanded such an execution, why didn't Josephus bother to write about it? Because Herod killed hundreds of people, including members of his own family. The drama throughout all of Judea immediately following the magi's visit was vengeful chaos, to say the least.

Herod was ill at the time the magi came to Jerusalem, and his health declined rapidly after they left. This was surely by the just hand of God. Herod had such a thirst for blood toward the end of his life, the Jews were counting down the days until he died. To prevent a celebration among the people upon his death, Herod summoned all the notable Jews from all over the kingdom and shut them in the hippodrome at Jericho. He ordered that the moment he died, all these officials were to be killed so there would be national mourning instead of a national festival.

Needless to say, no one carried out his demand. When Herod died, everyone he held captive was released. Again, all of this happened shortly after the magi visited. There was a lot going on in Judea apart from Herod's order to kill baby boys under the age of two in Bethlehem. We have no reason to doubt the truthfulness of Matthew's account. But we should certainly doubt claims that the number of the dead ranged in the tens to hundreds of thousands!

Our world today is no less chaotic than it was

back then. On December 12, 2014, a crazed gunman entered a public elementary school in Newtown, CT and killed 20 children between six and seven years old, as well as several adults, before taking his own life. America was stunned by this incredible tragedy, occurring less than two weeks before Christmas.

More shocking is the reality that three thousand pre-born children are murdered each day in America by the barbaric practice of abortion. An event like the Newtown massacre might receive a lot of coverage, and justifiably so. But where's the press regarding the thousands upon thousands of babies being killed in abortion clinics?

When we see all the evil going on in the world, we are tempted to ask, "Where's this peace on earth the angels talked about? Where's the goodwill toward men?"

At the start of the book of Habakkuk, the prophet cried to God, "O Lord, how long shall I cry for help, and you will not hear? Or cry to you 'Violence!' and you will not save? Why do you make me see iniquity, and why do you look at wrong? Destruction and violence are before me; strife and contention arise."

Then the Lord answered and said, "Look among the nations, and see; wonder and be astounded. For I am doing a work in your days that you would not believe if told" (Habakkuk 1:2-5).

God uses even violence to accomplish His perfect will, and the accomplishment is so beyond our imagination, we wouldn't believe it even if we were told beforehand what it was going to be. After all, God used the violent death of His Son, which He foreordained and brought about by His will (Acts 2:23, 4:28), to bring about the salvation of His people.

The peace that God gives us is infinitely greater than any peace we could find in this world. Because of our sin we were at enmity with God, and through Jesus Christ we have peace with God. Judgement is coming, but first a Savior came, that all who believe in Him will be saved. This world is evil because people are evil. God is good, and He has mercifully provided for our escape—through His Son, Jesus.

REFLECTION
This will be a little more difficult to reflect upon, but what is the saddest Christmas you can remember? How did God use the thing that caused you grief to eventually bring joy to your heart and glory to His name? It is always good to praise God, especially in the midst of trials. Sing together *I Heard the Bells On Christmas Day.*[36] Here are the lyrics:

> *I heard the bells on Christmas day*
> *Their old familiar carols play,*
> *And wild and sweet the words repeat*
> *Of peace on earth, good will to men.*

---

[36] Longfellow, Henry W. "I Heard the Bells on Christmas Day" *(Hymns of Grace).* Hymn 249.

I thought how, as the day had come,
The belfries of all Christendom
Had rolled along the unbroken song
Of peace on earth, good will to men.

And in despair I bowed my head:
"There is no peace on earth," I said,
"For hate is strong, and mocks the song
Of peace on earth, good will to men."

Then pealed the bells more loud and deep:
"God is not dead, nor does He sleep;
The wrong shall fail, the right prevail,
With peace on earth, good will to men."[37]

---

[37] This song was adapted from a poem written by Henry Wadsworth Longfellow, with music added later by John Calkin. Longfellow wrote his poem on Christmas day, 1863. His wife had died a couple of years earlier in a fire accident that also left Longfellow injured trying to save her. He was so badly burned he could not attend her funeral. Afterward, Longfellow fell into a deep depression. On Christmas day, 1862, he wrote in his journal, "A merry Christmas, say the children, but that is no more for me." The next year, his son Charles was badly wounded in battle during the Civil War. This was a war despised by Longfellow, a staunch abolitionist. He prayed it would end soon. While nursing his son back to health, he "heard the bells on Christmas day," restoring his hope in Christ and the promises in His word, inspiring him to write his famous poem.

Myth #10

The virgin birth is not important.

One of the classic Christmas spiritual songs goes like this:

The virgin Mary had a baby boy,
The virgin Mary had a baby boy,
The virgin Mary had a baby boy,
And they say that His name was Jesus.

Can you name that tune? You got it—*The Virgin Mary Had a Baby Boy.*

The gospel of Mathew says that Jesus' virgin birth was in fulfillment of what had been written by the prophet Isaiah: "Therefore the Lord Himself will give you a sign. Behold, the virgin shall conceive and bear a Son, and shall call His name Immanuel" (Isaiah 7:14).

The virgin birth is one of the most essential parts of the Christmas story. It's also one of the most shrugged at and scrutinized stories in the Bible. In his bestseller *God is Not Great,* atheist Christopher

Hitchens said, "Parthenogenesis," or virgin birth, "is not possible for human mammals." Uh, right, Chris—that's why it's called *miraculous!* Hitchens went on to say that even if the virgin birth were true, "it would not prove that the resulting infant had any divine power. Thus, and as usual, religion arouses suspicion by trying to prove too much."[38]

Andy Stanley, pastor of North Point megachurch in Atlanta, GA, shrugged at the virgin birth when he preached, "Matthew gives a version of the birth of Christ, Luke does, but Mark and John—they don't even mention it, and a lot has been made of that."

Stanley went on to say, "If someone can predict their own death and then their own resurrection, I'm not all that concerned about how they got into the world. Because the whole resurrection thing is so amazing, and in fact, you should know this— Christianity doesn't hinge on the truth or even the stories around the birth of Jesus. It really hinges on the resurrection of Jesus."[39]

Is Andy not amazed that the Old Testament prophets predicted Jesus' birth—specifically the virgin birth—and then it happened? Furthermore, as

---

[38] Hichens, Christopher. *God is Not Great: How Religion Poisons Everything* (Twelve, New York, 2007). Pg. 115.

[39] Stanley, Andy. *Who Needs Christmas? The World Did* (North Point Community Church, Atlanta, GA; December 3, 2016), sermon. http://northpoint.org/messages/who-needs-christmas/the-world-did/

we have seen, the prophets predicted the lineage, the time, and the exact place He would be born! And yet Andy thinks we shouldn't be concerned with those details, though it's literally the first event we read about in the New Testament!

Just how important is it to believe in the virgin birth of Christ? Well, if Jesus was not conceived by the Holy Spirit, then He had to have been conceived by the seed of a man. The Bible says that everyone who is born of Adam is born under the curse of Adam. All who are born of Adam inherit his sin nature, and the penalty for sin is death. As it says in Romans 5:12, "Therefore, just as sin came into the world through one man, and death through sin, and so death spread to all men because all sinned."

But because Jesus is conceived of the Holy Spirit, Jesus was born without sin. Remember the words of the angel to Mary: "The Holy Spirit will come upon you, and the power of the Most High will over-shadow you; therefore the child to be born will be called holy — the Son of God" (Luke 1:35). Why will the child be called holy? Because He will be without sin from the moment of His conception.

Remember what the angel said to Joseph: "Do not fear to take Mary as your wife, for that which is conceived in her is from the Holy Spirit. She will bear a son, and you shall call His name Jesus, for He will save His people from their sins" (Matt. 1:20-21). How will He be able to forgive sins? Because He will be the perfect, spotless sacrifice that is without blemish.

As John the Baptist said of Him, "Behold the Lamb of God, who takes away the sin of the world!" (John 1:29). Hebrews 9:22 says, "Indeed, under the law almost everything is purified with blood, and without the shedding of blood there is no forgiveness of sins." Under the Old Testament system of offering sacrifice, blood had to be shed to atone for sins, and the animal being offered had to be impeccable from birth. Jesus Christ is the fulfillment of that sacrificial system — the perfect man who laid His life down for sinful man.

Cynics are apt to say, "What a barbaric practice. God demanded the shedding of blood to appease His wrath?" We should be thankful that is all He demands. We frown on the Old Testament sacrifice of animals or balk at the notion that Jesus had to give His life because we think too much of ourselves and too little of God. Sacrifice is gross because sin is gross. Sin is an absolute stench in the nostrils of a holy God.

But Ephesians 5:2 says, "Christ loved us and gave Himself up for us, a fragrant offering and sacrifice to God." Jesus is the only one qualified to be such a sacrifice. He is impeccable — from His conception through His life and to His death on the cross. Jesus would not have been "the Lamb of God who takes away the sin of the world" if He had been born of the seed of man. Again, all who are born of Adam inherit

Adam's sin nature.

There's a theological understanding here referred to as *federal headship*. When you hear the word "federal," what do you think of? Probably the federal government, right? Under most modern systems of government, *federal headship* can be a concept difficult to grasp, so think of it from the perspective of a monarchy in Bible times, when nations were ruled by kings and emperors. When a king declared war on another king, both of their kingdoms were at war. Everyone in that kingdom was against everyone else in the other kingdom because their king, their federal head, had declared war.

When Adam sinned, every man declared war on God because, as Augustine argued, every man was present with Adam in the Garden of Eden. Adam is man's representative—our federal head. Of course, the folly in declaring war on God is that we will not win that fight. Who could possibly defeat God? Sin is cosmic treason against the High King of heaven, and we deserve to be annihilated for such rebellion.

But God gave His Son to die in our place. Jesus shed His blood on the cross as a propitiation for our sins. He satisfied the wrath of God burning against all unrighteousness (Romans 5:11). Everyone who has faith in Jesus Christ is no longer under the federal headship of Adam—the losing side. We're under the federal headship of Jesus—the victorious side. As a result, we've become heirs of the eternal kingdom of God—"heirs of God and fellow heirs with Christ" (Romans 8:17). By the grace of God, we're transformed from being treasonous criminals to fellow heirs!

All of this is possible because Jesus was virgin born. Had Jesus been born of the seed of man, then He would not have been without sin, and He would not have been a sacrifice who could atone for sin. Consider these words from Dr. Voddie Baucham:

> For those who say, 'The virgin birth, we can take it or we can leave it, it doesn't matter—all we need is Christ as our example.' No. If Christ was merely our example and there was no virgin birth, then He stands condemned because Adam is His federal head, as are all of those who come by natural generation. However, because of that virgin birth, Jesus Christ is not under that federal headship. This is why His impeccability matters. This is why it matters that Jesus did not sin.[40]

Much to Andy Stanley's chagrin, the virgin birth of Christ *is as important* as the resurrection of Christ. Without the virgin birth, there is no resurrection. It's because Christ's offering was perfectly received that He was resurrected. His body was conceived by the

---

[40] Buacham, Voddie. *Resurrection Life* (Orlando, FL; April 14, 2015), sermon on 1 Corinthians 15:35-58. https://you tu.be/U-Eyu3ppt4g

Holy Spirit, and His body was raised by the Holy Spirit. This was so we may also be raised by the Holy Spirit! Romans 8:11 says, "If the Spirit of Him who raised Jesus from the dead dwells in you, He who raised Christ Jesus from the dead will also give life to your mortal bodies through His Spirit who dwells in you."

Also, Andy's insistence that only two of the four gospels mention the virgin birth is incorrect. Perhaps the narrative appears in only Matthew and Luke, but Christ's virgin birth is mentioned elsewhere. In John 8:41, Jesus' critics mocked Him, *"We* were not born of sexual immorality!" It was known that Joseph was not the biological father of Jesus, but who could believe He was virgin born?

The doctrine of the virgin birth is not rejected because it has been disproved. It's rejected because of unbelief. After all, virgin birth is impossible, right? But as the angel Gabriel said to Mary, "Nothing will be impossible with God" (Luke 1:37).

REFLECTION

Read Romans 3:23-26. Who has sinned and fallen short of God's glory? Who will be justified? How will they be justified? What does it mean to be justified? Sing together this Christmas hymn *What Child is This.* Here are the lyrics:[41]

---

[41] Dix, William C. "What Child Is This?" *(Hymns of Grace).* Hymn 230.

What Child is this, who, laid to rest,
On Mary's lap is sleeping?
Whom angels greet with anthems sweet,
While shepherds watch are keeping?

Chorus:
This, this is Christ, the King,
Whom shepherds guard and angels sing:
Haste, haste to bring Him laud,
The Babe, the Son of Mary!

Why lies He in such mean estate,
Where ox and lamb are feeding?
Good Christian, fear: for sinners here
The silent Word is pleading.
(chorus)

So bring Him incense, gold, and myrrh,
Come, peasant, king to own Him.
The King of kings salvation brings;
Let loving hearts enthrone Him.
(chorus)

Myth #11

Mary the mother of Jesus was without sin.

Surely you've heard of the doctrine of the immaculate conception. The name of the doctrine was famously parodied on December 23, 1972, two days before Christmas, in an American football game between the Oakland Raiders and Pittsburg Steelers.

In the closing seconds of the game, the score 7-6 with the Raiders on top, the Steelers had one last shot to get the ball in the end zone. Quarterback Terry Bradshaw threw a pass to John Fuqua which was deflected off the helmet of Raiders safety Jack Tatum and into the hands of Steelers fullback Franco Harris, who ran the ball in for a touchdown. Game over. The Steelers won.

Okay, that's way too neat a description of what happened on the play. No one knows exactly what transpired. Maybe the ball went off Tatum's helmet, or maybe it went off Fuqua's hands. Maybe the ball hit the ground, or maybe Harris did scoop it up before it hit the turf. Television replay was not as sophisticated in the 1970s, and all these years later it's still difficult to tell.

Nevertheless, the "miracle" play lives on in football lore as the *Immaculate Reception.* It's a funny pun, but the name is a misnomer. The sportscaster for Pittsburg, Myron Cope, who coined the name thought the word "immaculate" was synonymous with "miracle." Actually, it means "pure," and that mess of a football play was anything but *pure.*

Whenever we hear mentioned the doctrine of the immaculate conception, it's often thought of as a reference to Jesus. After all, Jesus was born of a virgin, conceived by the Holy Spirit, and He was sinless, right? But the immaculate conception doesn't refer to Jesus at all — it refers to Mary.

The immaculate conception is a Roman Catholic doctrine which declares that Mary, like Jesus, was conceived in purity and was therefore untouched by the stain of original sin. Pope Pius IX proclaimed:

> We declare, pronounce, and define that the doctrine which holds that the most Blessed Virgin Mary, in the first instance of her conception, by a singular grace and privilege granted by Almighty God, in view of the merits of Jesus Christ, the Savior of the human race, was preserved free from all stain of original sin, is a doctrine revealed by God and therefore to be believed firmly and constantly by all the faithful.[42]

---

[42] Pope Pius IX, *Ineffabilis Deus,* 1870.

The Catholic church believes that for Jesus to be born without sin, Mary had to likewise be born without sin. Therefore, this doctrine was invented and introduced on December 8, 1854, now the date of the annual Feast of the Immaculate Conception. It was declared *Ex Cathedra* from the chair of St. Peter, meaning that the doctrine is to be held by all of Christ's church, and it is "irreformable."[43]

But the pope is not the head of the church — Christ is. Christ's word, the Bible, defines the church; the church does not define the Bible. What we have been told in Scripture contradicts the doctrine of the immaculate conception. Mary could not have been without sin, for "All have sinned and fall short of the glory of God" (Romans 3:23), and Jesus said, "No one is good except God alone" (Mark 10:18, Luke 18:19).

After Mary had given birth to Jesus, Joseph brought them to the temple to be purified according to the Law of God. Luke 2:22-24 says:

> And when the time came for their purification according to the Law of Moses, they brought Him up to Jerusalem to present Him to the Lord (as it is written in the Law of the Lord, "Every male who first opens the womb shall be called holy to the Lord") and to offer a sacrifice according to

---

[43] Pope Pius IX, *First Vatican Council*, Session 4 (July 18, 1870), Chapter 4, Section 9.

what is said in the Law of the Lord, "a pair of turtledoves or two young pigeons."

We read in Leviticus 12 that after a mother has given birth to a male child, she is to enter a time of purification for seven days. On the eighth day, the son is to be circumcised. The mother "shall continue for thirty-three days in the blood of her purifying. She shall not touch anything holy, nor come into the sanctuary, until the days of her purifying are completed" (v.4).

When the days of her purification are complete, she is to take sacrifices to the priest at the temple: "a lamb a year old for a burnt offering, and a pigeon or a turtledove for a sin offering." If she cannot afford a lamb, "then she shall take two turtledoves or two pigeons, one for a burnt offering and the other for a sin offering. And the priest shall make atonement for her, and she shall be clean."

This is exactly what we see Joseph and Mary doing in Luke 2:22-24. Mary would not have needed to offer up sacrifices to make atonement if she was sinless. Because Joseph and Mary were poor, they could not afford a lamb, so they had to offer "a pair of turtledoves or two young pigeons." Truth be told, *they did* come to the temple with a lamb—the Lamb of God, who is Jesus Christ!

When the angel Gabriel told Mary that she was going to have a son though she was a virgin, he also told her that her relative, Elizabeth, was expecting a son though she was beyond childbearing years. The child that Elizabeth was expecting was from the Lord. We would know him as John the Baptist.

Mary left Galilee and went to Judah to see Elizabeth. Upon greeting her, Elizabeth said to Mary, "Blessed are you among women, and blessed is the fruit of your womb! And why is this granted to me that the mother of my Lord should come to me? For behold, when the sound of your greeting came to my ears, the baby in my womb leaped for joy. And blessed is she who believed that there would be a fulfillment of what was spoken to her from the Lord" (Luke 1:42-45).

In Luke 1:46-55, we have what is known as the Song of Mary, when Mary rejoiced in the Lord after these words of Elizabeth's. At the start of the song, Mary sang:

My soul magnifies the Lord,
    and my spirit rejoices in God my Savior,
for He has looked on the humble
estate of His servant.
    For behold, from now on all generations
    will call me blessed;
for He who is mighty has done
great things for me,
    and holy is His name.

Notice that Mary referred to God as her "Savior." Mary, like you and me, needed a Savior. The child she gave birth to died for her sins as well, and she lived to see that day. She was also among the women who first found the empty tomb when Jesus rose from the grave (Mark 16:1), and she was in the upper room when the Holy Spirit came upon the apostles on the day of Pentecost (Acts 1:14). Mary was indeed a blessed woman. But she was not sinless.

The doctrine of the immaculate conception must be rejected outright for it renders the doctrine of the virgin birth meaningless. If God made Mary sinless though she wasn't virgin born, what difference does it make if Jesus was virgin born? If the doctrine of the immaculate conception falls, so does the so-called "chair of St. Peter." If the papacy falls, so goes the Catholic church.

As we're told in 1 Timothy 2:5-6, "For there is one God, and there is one mediator between God and men, the man Christ Jesus, who gave Himself as a ransom for all, which is the testimony given at the proper time."

The "all" Christ gave Himself for includes Mary. The "one mediator between God and men" is only Christ.

REFLECTION
Sing this hymn together, *I Lay My Sins on Jesus.* Talk about it when you are finished. Here are the lyrics:

I lay my sins on Jesus,
The spotless Lamb of God;
He bears them all and frees us
From the accursed load.
I bring my guilt to Jesus,
To wash my crimson stains
White in His blood most precious,
Till not a spot remains.

I lay my wants on Jesus.
All fullness dwells in Him;
He heals all my diseases;
He doth my soul redeem.
I lay my griefs on Jesus,
My burdens and my cares,
He from them all releases;
He all my sorrows shares.

I long to be like Jesus,
Meek, loving, lowly, mild;
I long to be like Jesus,
The Father's holy Child;
I long to be with Jesus,
Amid the heavenly throng;
To sing with saints His praises,
To learn the angels' song.[44]

---

[44] Bonar, Horatius. "I Lay My Sins on Jesus" (*Hymns of Grace*). Hymn 269.

Myth #12

Matthew and Luke's genealogies of Jesus contradict each other.

The gospel of Matthew starts like this: "The book of the genealogy of Jesus Christ, the Son of David, the son of Abraham" (Matthew 1:1). What follows is a genealogy that begins with Abraham, then traces fourteen generations to King David, follows a royal line of fourteen generations all the way up to the Jewish exile into the hands of the Babylonians, and finally marks fourteen more generations to "Joseph, the husband of Mary, of whom Jesus was born, who is called Christ" (v.16).

In the third chapter of the book of Luke, we have a somewhat different genealogy. While Matthew's goes from Abraham to Jesus, Luke starts with Jesus and goes all the way back to Adam, the first man. Luke's genealogy is also not as structured—it's just a continuous list of names. And many of those names are not on Matthew's list. From Abraham to David, the two genealogies are alike. But from David to Jesus, the genealogies are almost totally different.

Genealogies were very important to the Jews. The Old Testament is full of them, most notably 1 and 2 Chronicles. A person's genealogy helped to establish heritage, inheritance, legitimacy, and entitlements. Given that both Matthew and Luke had access to extremely detailed records of Jesus' lineage, why do their two genealogies come out so different?

The reason these genealogies are different is because Matthew traces Jesus' ancestry according to direct descendance, while Luke traces Jesus' ancestry according to Levirate marriage. Matthew 1:16 says Jacob is "the father of Joseph the husband of Mary, of whom Jesus was born, who is called Christ." Luke 3:23 says, "Jesus, when He began His ministry, was about thirty years of age, being the son (as was supposed) of Joseph, the son of Heli." According to Matthew, Joseph's father is Jacob; but according to Luke, Joseph's father is Heli.

It's not uncommon for Jews to have more than one name—for example, the Apostle Peter was also called Simon; the Apostle Paul was also called Saul; Matthew himself was known as Levi. Is it possible then that Heli and Jacob are actually the same person but with different names?

No, because Heli and Jacob do not have the same father. As we continue up the family trees, Jacob's father was Matthan while Heli's father was Matthat.

But wait—the names Matthat and Matthan aren't that different. They're just one letter off from each other. Could it be possible that Matthat and Matthan are the same person? No, because Matthat and Matthan have different fathers, too. Matthat's father is Levi, while Matthan's father is Eleazar. When we trace the two genealogies of Joseph back seven generations, the list looks like this:

Matthew's	Luke's
Jacob	Heli
Matthan	Matthat
Eleazar	Levi
Elihud	Melchi
Achim	Jannai
Zadok	Joseph
Azor	Mattathias

It's almost as if we're climbing two different family trees. The two lists don't converge until we get to King David. At the very least, we could say that Matthew and Luke agree Jesus was descended from David, but surely several Jews could have said they were descended from David. The problem is compounded when we confess the word of God is without error, and yet it looks here as if there's error. Why do Matthew and Luke seem to be so confused as to who Joseph's father was?

A third century writer named Africanus said that he understood the answer as given to him from the kinsmen of our Lord. This means he spoke with those who were descended from Jesus' half-siblings, the children of Mary, Jesus' mother. That's quite a resource! The words of Africanus were recorded by the Christian historian Eusebius in his fourth century work *Ecclesiastical History*. Here is what Eusebius wrote according to Africanus:

> As Joseph is our proposed end, we are to show how it happened that each of these two (Jacob and Heli) is recorded as his father; also how it happened that these two, Jacob and Heli, were brothers; and, moreover how the fathers of these Matthan and [Matthat] being of different families, are proved to be the grandfathers of Joseph.
>
> Matthan and [Matthat], having married in succession the same woman, had children who were brothers by the same mother—as the law did not prohibit a widow, whether she became such by divorce or the death of her husband, to marry again. Matthan, therefore, who traces his lineage from Solomon, first had Jacob by Estha, for this is her name, as known by tradition. Matthan dying, and [Matthat], who traces his descent from Nathan, though he was of the same tribe, but of another family, having, as before said, married her, had a son, Heli. Thus, then, we shall find the two of different families, Jacob and Heli, brothers by the same mother.

Of these the one Jacob, on the death of his brother, marrying his widow, became the father of a third, Joseph, his son both by nature and calculation. Wherefore it is written: Jacob begot Joseph. But, according to the law, he was the son of Heli; for Jacob, being his brother, raised up seed to him.[45]

Are you with me so far?

Toward the end of chapter 7, Eusebius summed up Africanus' explanation like this: "Matthan, whose lineage is from Nathan, by marrying the widow of the former had Heli. Hence, Heli and Jacob were brothers by the same mother. Heli dying childless, Jacob raised up seed to him having Joseph, according to nature belonging to himself, but by the law to Heli. Thus Joseph was the son of both."

This is the law of Levirate marriage. Beginning in Deuteronomy 25:5, we read, "If brothers dwell together, and one of them dies and has no son, the wife of the dead man shall not be married outside the family to a stranger. Her husband's brother shall go in to her and take her as his wife and perform the duty of a husband's brother to her. And the first son whom she bears shall succeed to the name of this dead brother, that his name may not be blotted out of Israel."

According to the law in Israel, when a man and a

---

[45] Eusebius, *Ecclesiastical History.* 1.7.

woman got married, and before they had children something tragic happened and the husband died childless, the woman, now a widow, must not remarry outside the family. She must marry her husband's brother, who must fulfill the duty of a brother-in-law with her. The first son she gives birth to must carry on the name of the dead brother so that the dead brother's name will not be blotted out of Israel. The child is an inheritor of everything that belonged to the dead brother, including his name. The living brother begat the child, but the child is heir to the dead brother according to the law.

Matthew 1:16 says, "and Jacob the father of Joseph the husband of Mary, of whom Jesus was born, who is called Christ." In the Greek form of this verse, we find the word ἐγέννησεν *(egennesen)* which means "begat." That same word does not appear in Luke's genealogy, where it simply says, "Joseph, the son of Heli" (Luke 3:23). According to Matthew, Jacob is Joseph's biological father. According to Luke, Heli is Joseph's father by law.

Perhaps this seems confusing, but it shows that Matthew and Luke do not contradict each other. It is instead a testament to the seamless perfection of Scripture and the foreordained plan of our sovereign God. Jesus was begotten *and* He was seed who was raised up *and* He was adopted. Remember, Jesus is not the flesh-and-blood son of Joseph — He is Joseph's adopted son. At the same time, Joseph is a direct descendent of Jacob, but a legal descendent of Heli.

Jesus is the adopted son of Joseph, who is the descendent of Jacob, but he is the son of Heli by law. In even these seemingly minute ways, Jesus Christ is the fulfillment of all the Law and the prophets. Jesus said, "Do not think that I have come to abolish the Law of the Prophets; I have not come to abolish them but to fulfill them" (Matthew 5:17). We see this accomplished even in His genealogy.

Regarding the genealogies of Christ, R.C. Sproul said, "What this beginning lacks in literary punch it makes up for in theological significance. Among other things, the genealogical tables of the New Testament place the gospel squarely on the plane of history. Jesus was born 'in the fullness of time' — His ministry is defined and interpreted against the background of Old Testament history."[46]

REFLECTION

Galatians 4:6 says that as sons and daughters of God, "God has sent the Spirit of His Son into our hearts crying, 'Abba! Father!'" (see also Romans 8:15). What does adoption mean? Do you know anyone who is adopted? How are we adopted into the family of God? How can we show the same spirit of love to one another that God has shown to us? Sing together

---

[46] Sproul, R.C. *Tracing the Genealogy of Jesus* (Ligonier.org, Dec. 20, 2009). https://www.ligonier.org/blog/tracing-genealogy-jesus/

the song *O Holy Night*. Here are the lyrics to two of the verses:

O holy night! The stars are brightly shining
It is the night of the dear Savior's birth.
Long lay the world in sin and error pining,
Till He appeared and the soul felt its worth
A thrill of hope, the weary world rejoices,
For yonder breaks a new and glorious morn!
Fall on your knees! O hear the angel voices!
O night divine, O night when Christ was born!
O night divine, O night when Christ was born!

Truly He taught us to love one another;
His law is love and His gospel is peace.
Chains shall He break, for the slave is our brother,
And in His name all oppression shall cease.
Sweet hymns of joy in grateful chorus raise we;
Let all within us praise His holy name.
Christ is the Lord! O praise his name forever!
His power and glory evermore proclaim!
His power and glory evermore proclaim![47]

---

[47] Dwight, John S. "O Holy Night!" *(Hymns of Grace).* Hymn 240.

Myth #13

Matthew's genealogy traces Joseph's ancestry while Luke's genealogy traces Mary's.

There's another popular explanation for why Matthew's genealogy of Jesus and Luke's genealogy are different. In fact, this is the most common appeal among Bible teachers defending the truthfulness of God's word. The reason the genealogies differ, they will say, is because Matthew traced after Joseph's ancestry while Luke traced after Mary's.

In *The Jesus Answer Book,* John MacArthur notes, "In Matthew, the genealogy is paternal, going through Jesus' earthly father, Joseph; and Joseph's father, Jacob; back to David. In Luke, the genealogy is maternal, going through Jesus' mother, Mary; and Mary's father, Heli; back to David."[48]

Now, I hate to pick on John MacArthur, and I offer this critique with a humble spirit. I have great admiration for the man who has committed decades

---

[48] MacArthur, John; *The Jesus Answer Book* (Thomas Nelson, Nashville, TN; 2014). Pg. 8.

of faithful service to preaching the full council of God. It is out of my respect for Pastor MacArthur and in keeping with his own commitment to rightly handle the word of truth (2 Timothy 2:15) that I must say — albeit modestly — his answer to this conundrum is incorrect.

The reason the two genealogies are different is not because one is tracing the genealogy of Joseph while the other is looking at Mary. Luke's genealogy doesn't even mention Mary, but both genealogies do mention Joseph as the legal earthly father of Jesus. The maternal argument also doesn't make sense from a Jewish standpoint since genealogies were traced through the father, not the mother.

As I conveyed in the previous chapter, Matthew traces Jesus' line according to direct descendance, whereas Luke traces Jesus' line according to the law. But why? What difference does it make? Why can't the genealogies just be the same? Then we don't have to stir up such questions as this one, and I don't have to differ with such a great teacher whom I respect!

Well, like I said, I believe one of the reasons the genealogies are set up differently is to show by God's providence how Jesus has indeed fulfilled every dot and tittle of all the Law and the prophets. But there's another reason these genealogies differ, and that has to do with each respective author's intentions.

Matthew was writing to a Jewish audience. He started with genealogy to show that Jesus Christ is a

Jew in the line of Abraham, Isaac, Jacob, and Judah. He also showed that Jesus is a descendent of King David, which makes Him an inheritor to the throne of Israel. This was necessary to establish that Jesus is the fulfillment of the covenant that God made with David.

The first place we read of this covenant is in 2 Samuel 7. Through the prophet Nathan, the Lord said to David, "Your house and your kingdom shall be made sure forever before me. Your throne shall be established forever" (2 Samuel 7:16). In Psalm 18:50 we read that God "shows steadfast love to his anointed, to David and his offspring forever."

How has God shown steadfast love to David and his offspring forever? By fulfilling the covenant He made with David, which God accomplished through Jesus Christ, a descendent of David and enthroned in heaven forever.

Regarding the coming of Christ, Isaiah 9:7 says, "Of the increase of His government and of peace there will be no end, on the throne of David and over His kingdom, to establish it and to uphold it with justice and with righteousness from this time forth and forevermore."

How is it that the throne of David has no end? Because Jesus, God incarnate, who put on flesh and dwelt among us, came to earth born in the line of King David, according to the Scriptures. After He died on the cross and rose again from the grave, He ascended back to His Father in heaven.

Hebrews 1:3 says, "After making purification for sins, He sat down at the right hand of the Majesty on high," and Hebrews 12:2 says that Jesus is "seated at the right hand of the throne of God." Ephesians 1:20 says that God "raised Him from the dead and seated Him at His right hand in the heavenly places."

Matthew's genealogy shows how Jesus, David's descendent and the eternal King who sits enthroned in heaven, is the fulfillment of the Davidic covenant. This was incredibly significant to a Jew. It is no less significant for us today, since all who have faith in Christ "are Abraham's offspring, heirs according to promise" (Galatians 3:29). We have the whole Bible, "the prophetic word more fully confirmed" (2 Peter 1:19).

While Matthew's audience was Jewish, Luke's was Gentile. As stated earlier, Luke addressed his gospel to a single man: Theophilus. The name is obviously Greek (Greek and Gentile are often used interchangeably in the New Testament). It's also quite symbolic when you consider that the meaning of the name is "loved of God" or "friend of God."

Matthew traced Jesus' lineage through David to Abraham to show that Jesus is a true Jew and the rightful heir to the throne of David. But Luke went beyond that through David and Abraham to Adam. In doing so, Luke means to convey to the reader that Jesus Christ is the second Adam.

Luke was a physician and a missionary friend of the Apostle Paul. The gospel as Luke wrote it is essentially the gospel the way Paul preached it. Explaining that Jesus Christ is the last Adam was common to Paul's teaching. To the Corinthians, Paul wrote:

> For as by a man came death, by a man has come also the resurrection of the dead. For as in Adam all die, so also in Christ shall all be made alive... Thus it is written, 'The first man Adam became a living being'; the last Adam became a life-giving spirit... The first man was from the earth, a man of dust; the second man is from heaven. As was the man of dust, so also are those who are of the dust, and as is the man of heaven, so also are those who are of heaven. Just as we have borne the image of the man of dust, we shall also bear the image of the man of heaven. (1 Corinthians 15:21-22, 45, 47-49).

Just as all who are under Adam are born into unrighteousness, so all who are under Christ are born *again* into righteousness. Just as all who are born of Adam will die, so all who are born *again* in Christ will live. Where Adam had failed, Christ has succeeded.

Through Matthew's genealogy, we have come to recognize that Jesus Christ is the fulfillment of the

Davidic covenant. Through Luke's genealogy, we come to recognize that Jesus Christ is the last Adam and a Savior for all men.

To quote again from John MacArthur and give him the last teaching word here, he says, "You may skip the genealogy when you read the Christmas story aloud. But don't overlook its message of grace, which after all is the heart of the Christmas story: God in His mercy doing for sinners what they cannot do for themselves—mending broken lives and restoring shattered hopes. That's why He came—to save His people from their sins."[49]

REFLECTION

Do you know the names of your grandparents? Your great grandparents? How about your great, *great* grandparents? Is your family mostly Christian, or do you have a lot of unbelievers in your family? What is a way that you could share the gospel with them? Sing this Christmas hymn together, *Lo, How a Rose E'er Blooming*. Here are the lyrics:

> *Lo, how a Rose e'er blooming*
> *From tender system hath sprung!*
> *Of Jesse's lineage coming*
> *As men of old have sung.*
> *It came, a flower bright*

---

[49] MacArthur, John; *Truth for Today: A Daily Touch of God's Grace* (Thomas Nelson, Nashville, TN; 2001). Pg. 380.

Amid the cold of winter
When half-gone was the night.

Isaiah 'twas foretold it,
The Rose I have in mind;
With Mary we behold it,
The virgin mother kind.
To show God's love aright
She bore to men a Savior
When half-gone was the night.

This Flower, whose fragrance tender
With sweetness fills the air,
Dispels with glorious splendor
The darkness everywhere.
True man, yet very God,
From sin and death He saves us
And lightens every load.[50]

---

[50] Baker, Theodore; Krauth Spaeth. "Lo, How a Rose E'er Blooming" *(Hymns of Grace)*. Hymn 220.

Myth #14
Mary is the New Eve.

At the start of the Christmas story, an angel spoke to Mary and told her that the fruit of her womb would be called the Son of God. At the start of the creation story, a fallen angel spoke to Eve and told her the fruit of the tree would make her like God.

It's in Genesis 3:1 that we are first introduced to that ancient serpent called Satan. The serpent said to Eve, "Did God actually say, 'You shall not eat of any tree in the garden?'"

Eve replied, "We may eat of the fruit of the trees in the garden, but God said, 'You shall not eat of the fruit of the tree that is in the midst of the garden, neither shall you touch it, lest you die.'"

But the serpent said to the woman, "You will not surely die. For God knows that when you eat of it your eyes will be opened, and you will be like God, knowing good and evil."

So the woman took the fruit of the tree and she at it. She also gave some to her husband, Adam, who was with her, and he ate. Then the eyes of both were opened, and they knew they were exposed and naked. Adam and Eve sowed fig leaves into loincloths to try and hide their nakedness.

When they heard God walking in the Garden in the cool of the day, they ran and hid from Him. The Lord called to Adam and said, "Where are you?"

In the worst game of hide-and-seek ever, Adam replied, "I heard the sound of you in the garden, and I was afraid, because I was naked, and I hid myself."

God said, "Who told you that you were naked? Have you eaten of the tree of which I commanded you not to eat?"

Adam said, "The woman whom you gave to be with me, she gave me the fruit of the tree, and I ate!"

Then the Lord God said to the woman, "What is this that you have done?"

She said, "The serpent deceived me, and I ate."

So the Lord said to the serpent, "Because you have done this, cursed are you above all livestock and above all beasts of the field; on your belly you shall go, and dust you shall eat all the days of your life. I will put enmity between you and the woman, and between your offspring and her offspring; He shall bruise your head, and you shall bruise His heal."

God also cursed Eve and all women after her to experience pain in childbearing and strife with her husband. Adam was cursed to fruitless labor and after a life of that would come death. The ground would be against him, for all of creation would be subjected to futility. Mankind was now unholy, cast from paradise and from the presence of God. Every descendent of man would likewise inherit the curse and Adam's sin nature.

But consider again that statement God made to the serpent. He said, "I will put enmity between you and the woman, and between your offspring and her offspring; He shall bruise your head, and you shall bruise His heal" (Genesis 3:15).

This is referred to as the *protoevangelium,* the first gospel proclamation in the Bible — the offspring of the woman would crush the head of the snake. Given that this passage is a prophecy concerning Christ, doesn't it make sense to say that Mary is the new Eve? After all, if Christ is the Last Adam, can't we conclude there was a last Eve?

Any parallels between Mary and Eve should be considered mere allegory, for the Bible never refers to Mary as Eve. The doctrine of the New Eve is yet another extra-biblical concoction, more common to the Roman Catholic and Eastern Orthodox churches.

According to Pope Paul VI, "We believe that the Holy Mother of God, the New Eve, Mother of the Church, continues in heaven to exercise her maternal role on behalf of the members of Christ."[51]

---

[51] Pope Paul VI, *The Credo of the People of God* (Pauline Books & Media, 1968). 16 Pgs.

But remember, Mary was not the "Holy Mother of God." The doctrine of the New Eve needs the doctrine of the immaculate conception in order to make sense, and as we've examined, the immaculate conception is a false teaching. Mary is also not the "Mother of the Church." The Apostle Paul said to the church in Galatia, "The Jerusalem above is free, and she is our mother" (Galatians 4:26).

The New Eve doctrine also relies upon a doctrine called the Assumption of Mary, another Catholic teaching which declares Mary did not die but was taken up bodily into heaven. This dogma wasn't invented until Pope Pius XII in 1950. According to Catholic Answers:

> The key to understanding all of these graces is Mary's role as the New Eve, which the early Fathers proclaimed so forcefully. Because she is the New Eve, she, like the New Adam, was born immaculate, just as the First Adam and Eve were created immaculate. Because she is the New Eve, she is mother of the New Humanity (Christians), just as the first Eve was the mother of humanity. And, because she is the New Eve, she shares the fate of the New Adam. Whereas the First Adam and Eve died and went to dust, the New Adam and Eve were lifted up physically into heaven.[52]

---

[52] https://www.catholic.com/tract/mary-full-of-grace

None of this is found in the Bible, but it also was not "proclaimed so forcefully" by the early church Fathers as the Catholic apologists would have you believe. Justin Martyr, Irenaeus, and Tertullian are among the scholars cited as being the first to teach Mary was the New Eve, but they wrote allegorically, not literally. None of them used the term "New Eve," none said Mary was without sin, and none believed Mary ascended bodily into heaven. All of these are doctrines that are more recent inventions.

Some have tried to argue that Jesus referred to Mary as Eve. In John 2:1-11, we read about the wedding feast at Cana where Jesus performed His first miracle—turning water into wine. When the wine first ran out, Mary said to Jesus, "They have no wine." Jesus replied, "Woman, what does this have to do with me? My hour has not yet come."

Apologists of the New Eve theory say that when Jesus called His mother "Woman," this was the same as calling her Eve. However, "Woman" happened to be a polite and respectful address in first century Galilee, much like we might say something like Ma'am or Miss or Madam. Two chapters later, Jesus addressed the Samaritan woman at the well as "Woman" (John 4:21), so it was not an address unique to Mary.

To be theologically consistent, it doesn't make sense to call Mary the New Eve. Jesus is "the last Adam." Who was Adam's wife? Certainly not his mother. It was Eve. Who is the bride of Christ? According to holy writ, that would be the church.[53] In Ephesians 5:22-28, the Bible says:

> Wives, submit to your own husbands, as to the Lord. For the husband is the head of the wife even as Christ is the head of the church, His body, and is Himself its Savior. As the church submits to Christ, so also wives should submit in everything to their husbands.
>
> Husbands, love your wives as Christ loved the church and gave Himself up for her, that He might sanctify her, having cleansed her by the washing of water with the word, so that He might present the church to Himself in splendor, without spot or wrinkle or any such thing, that she might be holy and without blemish. In the same way husbands should love their wives as their own bodies. He who loves his wife loves himself.

Consider this: When God asked Adam if he had eaten of the tree God told him not to eat from, what was Adam's reply? He said, "The woman *whom you gave to be with me,* she gave me the fruit of the tree, and I ate." Adam threw his wife under the bus, and blamed God for it.

---

[53] See also Matthew 25:1-13; Mark 2:19-20; John 3:29 and 14:1-3, and Revelation 18:23, 19:7, 21:2, 9-10, and 22:17.

What should Adam's response have been? When Adam saw that his wife had eaten the forbidden fruit, he shouldn't have done likewise. Remember, Adam "was with her, and he ate" (Genesis 3:6).

What he *should have done* was go before God and say, "Whatever her punishment is supposed to be, give it to me instead. I will take it for her." Since Adam would not have eaten the fruit as Eve did, Adam would have been without sin. God would have received Adam's offering of himself, and Eve would have been forgiven by Adam's sacrifice.

Of course, that's not what Adam did for Eve, but that is what Christ has done for us. Romans 5:8 says, "But God shows His love for us in that while we were still sinners, Christ died for us." Now having been justified by His grace, we are also being sanctified by His love, "by the washing of water with the word, so that He might present the church to Himself in splendor."

REFLECTION

How has the love that Christ has shown to us teach us to love each other? How can it change a marriage? How can it change a family? Can you think of what ways His love affects any other relationships we have? Sing the following hymn together, *I Will Sing of My Redeemer.* Here are the lyrics:[54]

---

[54] Bliss, Philip. "I Will Sing of My Redeemer" *(Hymns of Grace).* Hymn 210.

I will sing of my Redeemer
And His wondrous love to me;
On the cruel cross He suffered
From the curse to set me free.

Chorus:
Sing, O sing of my Redeemer,
With His blood He purchased me.
On the cross He sealed my pardon,
Paid the debt and made me free.

I will tell the wondrous story
How, my lost estate to save,
In His boundless love and mercy
He the ransom freely gave.
(chorus)

I will praise my dear Redeemer;
His triumphant power I'll tell,
How the victory He giveth
Over sin and death and hell.
(chorus)

I will sing of my Redeemer
And His heavenly love for me;
He from death to life hath brought me,
Son of God, with Him to be.
(chorus)

Myth #15
Jesus was an only child.

When Mary became pregnant, Joseph thought that she had been unfaithful to him, and he resolved to divorce her quietly. But an angel of the Lord appeared to him in a dream and said, "Joseph, son of David, do not fear to take Mary as your wife, for that which is conceived in her is from the Holy Spirit. She will bear a son, and you shall call His name Jesus, for He will save His people from their sins."

In Matthew 2:14-15, we read, "When Joseph woke from sleep, he did as the angel of the Lord commanded him: he took his wife, but knew her not until she had given birth to a son. And he called his name Jesus."

Of course, Mary was a virgin when she became with child, for what was conceived in her was from the Holy Spirit. For Matthew to say that Joseph "knew her not *until* she had given birth to a son" implies that eventually they did consummate their marriage—or as I put it earlier, Joseph *knew his wife biblically.* Wink, wink.

Still, there is a strain of heterodoxy that insists on a doctrine of the perpetual virginity of Mary — that Mary never had other children after Jesus, nor did Joseph ever *know* his wife, and she remained a virgin for the rest of her life. As popular as this doctrine is within Catholicism, it is also supported by the Orthodox church and affirmed among Anglicans and some Protestants.

Later in Matthew, Jesus came to His hometown of Nazareth and preached there in the synagogue. The people said, "Where did this man get this wisdom and these mighty works? Is not this the carpenter's son? Is not His mother called Mary? And are not His brothers James and Joseph and Simon and Judas? Are not all His sisters with us? Where then did this man get all these things?" (Matthew 13:54-56).

This is a clear reference to Jesus' half-brothers and sisters. Joseph is even mentioned and Jesus' mother, Mary. How could this mean anything other than Mary had other children with Joseph? Not only are Jesus' siblings mentioned in all four gospels, they're mentioned in the book of Acts, by the Apostle Paul in at least two of his epistles, and two of Jesus' half-brothers wrote New Testament books (James and Jude).

Oh, but apologists for the perpetual virginity of Mary will go right on insisting these were *not* Mary's biological children. As early as the fourth century, St.

Jerome said these children of Mary were actually cousins, born to Mary of Cleopas, Jesus' aunt and His mother's sister. Since Mary of Nazareth and Mary of Cleopas were sisters and shared the exact same first name, it's understandable to see how someone could get confused.

Jerome further insisted that the Greek word ἀδελφοὶ *(adelphois)*, translated "brothers" in Matthew 13:55, could also mean cousins and not biological children.[55] Fifth century theologian Augustine of Hippo also believed this. Another popular theory is that Joseph had another wife before Mary, and these siblings mentioned in the gospels and by Paul were Joseph's former wife's children.

The latter theory is a theological travesty. If Jesus was not Joseph's first son, he would not be heir to the throne of David. The former theory is also bunk. The use of *adelphois* in the New Testament never means anything other than blood-related kinsmen. Of course, the word is also used to describe spiritual brethren in the church, but the saints are all related by blood — we are brothers and sisters redeemed by the blood of Christ!

It is plainly stated in the Scriptures that Jesus had half-siblings born to Mary and Joseph. Why would anyone feel the need to defy this and insist on the

---

[55] Murphy-Gill, Meghan. "Did Jesus Have Brothers and Sisters?" *(U.S. Catholic*, Vol. 78, No. 12; December, 2013). Pg. 46.

perpetual virginity of Mary? What possible value could there be in that doctrine? The answer is none. But there are those who believe virginity is somehow pure, while sex—even within marriage—makes one unclean. At the heart of the doctrine of the perpetual virginity of Mary is an incorrect understanding of human sexuality the way God made it.

John Wesley, the founder of Methodism, said, "the Blessed Virgin Mary, who, as well after as before she brought Him forth, continued a pure and unspotted Virgin."[56] This conveys two things: 1) that a person who is *not* a virgin *can't be* "pure and unspotted;" 2) that living as a virgin is a higher order than marriage.

First of all, Jesus said that if anyone lusts after a woman, he has committed adultery with her in his heart (Matthew 5:28). So sexual immorality is not just about what one does with their body. You can be physically a virgin yet sexually impure. Regarding the second point, the Bible says nothing about virginity being a higher calling than marriage. What the Bible does say is that prohibiting marriage for anyone is the teaching of demons (1 Timothy 4:1-3).

Now, I don't think Wesley was saying that in order to remain pure one must not get married, but it's still his poor theology concerning a biblical ethic

---

[56] Holden, H.W., *John Wesley in Company with High Churchmen*, Second Ed. (Church Press Company, London; 1870). Pg. 119.

of sexuality that led him to say what he said about the perpetual virginity of Mary.

In first century Corinth, a kind of thinking had developed among some of these new Christians that in order to be holy, they had to stop having sex altogether—even with their spouses. They wrote to the Apostle Paul, "It is good for a man not to have sexual relations with a woman" (1 Corinthians 7:1). Paul responded to them this way:

[Now] because of the temptation to sexual immorality, each man should have his own wife and each woman her own husband. The husband should give to his wife her conjugal rights, and likewise the wife to her husband. For the wife does not have authority over her own body, but the husband does. Likewise, the husband does not have authority over his own body, but the wife does. Do not deprive one another, except perhaps by agreement for a limited time, that you may devote yourselves to prayer; but then come together again, so that Satan may not tempt you because of your lack of self-control.

Given that this was a command from the apostle and therefore from the Lord, here's what we must realize—Had Mary *not* consummated her marriage with Joseph and slept with him, she would have been sinning against God and rejecting His created order for marriage. Also, poor Joseph!

Jesus said, "Have you not read that He who created them from the beginning made them male and female, and said, 'Therefore a man shall leave his father and his mother and hold fast to his wife, and the two shall become one flesh'? So they are no longer two but one flesh. What therefore God has joined together, let man not separate" (Matthew 19:4-6).

Jesus quoted from the creation story in Genesis. After God made Eve from the rib of Adam, Scripture says, "Therefore a man shall leave his father and his mother and hold fast to his wife, and they shall become one flesh" (Genesis 2:24). To the man and the woman, God said, "Be fruitful and multiply and fill the earth and subdue it." He looked at all that He created, "and behold, it was very good" (Genesis 1:26-31).

Marriage is the taking of two people, a man and a woman, from two different families and making one new family: "the two shall become one flesh." The purpose of family is to "be fruitful and multiply." This is God's intention for marriage, which He created. So to insist that Mary had only Jesus and never had any other children, but that she remained a virgin the rest of her life and this was a more pure calling, is to make an argument against God's created order and His intention for marriage.

The kind of purity we've been called to is to

abstain not from sex but from sexual *immorality.* Sex is meant for a husband and wife, and any kind of sexual activity outside of that covenant is sin. Sex is good when it is enjoyed the way God meant for it to be enjoyed. We read in Hebrews 13:4, "Let marriage be held in honor among all, and let the marriage bed be undefiled, for God will judge the sexually immoral and adulterous."

Jesus was the firstborn child, but He was not the only child. The Scripture is clear that Mary had children with Joseph, but this does not make her any less blessed or any less a woman to be admired. The purity she had was not because of her abstinence, but because of her Savior, who cleanses us by His grace.

REFLECTION
What does it mean to be pure? How can we be made pure? How can we maintain purity? Sing together the hymn *Come, Thou Long-Expected Jesus.* Here are the lyrics:

Come, Thou long expected Jesus,
Born to set Thy people free;
From our fears and sins release us;
Let us find our rest in Thee.
Israel's strength and consolation,
Hope of all the earth Thou art;
Dear desire of every nation
Joy of every longing heart.

Born Thy people to deliver,
Born a child, and yet a King,
Born to reign in us forever,
Now Thy gracious kingdom bring.
By Thine own eternal Spirit
Rule in all our hearts alone;
By Thine all sufficient merit,
Raise us to Thy glorious throne.[57]

---

[57] Wesley, Charles. "Come, Thou Long-Expected Jesus" *(Hymns of Grace)*. Hymn 216.

Myth #16
Jesus is God the Father.

One of the most popular verses we read around Christmas is Isaiah 9:6, a prophecy concerning the coming of Christ: "For to us a child is born, to us a Son is given; and the government shall be upon His shoulder, and His name shall be called Wonderful Counselor, Mighty God, Everlasting Father, Prince of Peace." This verse has made it into many Christmas-themed songs, perhaps none more famous than Handel's *Messiah*.

Iconic baroque composer George Frideric Handel debuted his masterpiece *Messiah* on the stage of Musick Hall in Dublin, Ireland on April 13, 1742. The three-hour, 260-page oratorio was composed in an astonishing twenty-four days. Experienced musicians would struggle to merely copy the music in that amount of time. Ludwig Van Beethoven had called Handel "the greatest composer that ever lived."[58]

---

[58] 1. Kandell, Jonathan; "The Glorious History of Handel's Messiah" (*Smithsonian Magazine,* December, 2009).

Originally an Easter offering, *Messiah* has since become as thematic to the Christmas season as *Jingle Bells*.[59] *Messiah* is presented in three parts: the first prophesying the birth of Christ, the second exalting Jesus' sacrifice for mankind (concluding with the *Hallelujah* chorus), and the final section heralding His resurrection. It's in Part 1, Scene 3 where Handel incorporated the words from Isaiah 9:6.

Magnificent is Isaiah's description of our coming Christ and King—even more glorious when sung by a choir! But sometimes these sacred words can be so mangled by false teachers, it might sound on the tongues of heretics less like a grand choir and more like someone falling into an orchestra pit.

Isaiah 9:6 happens to be a favorite passage among Trinity-deniers, those who reject the understanding that our one God is three persons: Father, Son, and Holy Spirit. According to the historic confession, "All three are infinite and without beginning and are therefore one God, who is not to be divided in nature and being."[60]

---

[59] *Jingle Bells* was also not a Christmas song. It was written in 1850 by James Lord Pierpont to promote horse and sleigh drag racing in Boston. Look up the lyrics sometime. They're quite strange. *Jingle Bells* is also the first song ever broadcast from space, sung by pilots Walter Schirra and Thomas Stafford aboard the Gemini VI mission in 1965.

[60] The 1689 London Baptist Confession of Faith (in modern English), 2:3.

You can probably guess which part of Isaiah 9:6 the Trinity-deniers like to abuse—it's the part where Jesus is described as "Everlasting Father." They will take this out of context to argue that God the Father and the Son of God are the same person, and therefore God cannot be Triune.

Jesus is not God the Father. Rather, Jesus shows us the Father. John 1:18 says, "No one has ever seen God; the only God, who is at the Father's side, He has made Him known." Jesus said, "No one knows the Son except the Father, and no one knows the Father except the Son and anyone to whom the Son chooses to reveal Him" (Matthew 11:27).

In addition to showing us the Father, Jesus also gives the Holy Spirit, who testifies to the Father and the Son. Jesus said, "But when the Helper comes, whom I will send to you from the Father, the Spirit of truth, who proceeds from the Father, He will bear witness about me" (John 15:26). We read in 1 John 5:6 that "the Spirit is the one who testifies, because the Spirit is the truth."

If Jesus is not the Father, what is meant by Isaiah 9:6 where it says that He will be called "Everlasting Father"? Very simply, it means Jesus is our federal head in place of Adam. Before Christ, Adam was our federal head who brought death to us. In Christ, Jesus is our federal head who brings everlasting life to us.

These descriptors in Isaiah 9:6 are all attributes of

a great king. That's the context. Verse 7 says, "Of the increase of His government and of peace there will be no end, on the throne of David and over His kingdom, to establish it and to uphold it with justice and with righteousness from this time forth and forevermore."

In the kingdom of Christ, His people know Him by each of these names. Consider first that Jesus is called *Wonderful Counselor*. Isaiah says that the Lord "is wonderful in counsel and excellent in wisdom" (Isaiah 28:29). Psalm 33:11 says, "The counsel of the Lord stands forever, the plans of His heart to all generations." Job 12:13 says, "With God are wisdom and might; He has counsel and understanding."

Second, Jesus is called *Mighty God*. Psalm 50:1 says, "The Mighty One, God the Lord, speaks and summons the earth from the rising of the sun to its setting." When we read such exalting passages, it is specifically Christ whom we are reading about. In heaven for all eternity, we will sing, "Hallelujah! For the Lord our God the Almighty reigns" (Revelation 19:6).

Third, Jesus is called *Everlasting Father*. Psalm 103:13 says, "As a father shows compassion to his children, so the Lord shows compassion to those who fear Him." Deuteronomy 8:5 says, "Know then in your heart that, as a father disciplines his son, the Lord your God disciplines you." Jesus said, "Those whom I love, I reprove and discipline, so be zealous and repent" (Revelation 3:19).

Lastly, Jesus is the *Prince of Peace*. Psalm 46:9 says, "He makes wars cease to the end of the earth; He breaks the bow and shatters the spear; He burns the chariots with fire." Jesus said to His disciples, "Peace I leave with you; my peace I give to you. Not as the world gives do I give to you. Let not your hearts be troubled, neither let them be afraid" (John 14:27). Through faith in Jesus Christ, you have a "peace that surpasses all understanding," and "the God of peace will be with you" (Philippians 4:7, 9).

All four of these titles in Isaiah 9:6 are also exemplified in Psalm 68:

- *Wonderful Counselor:* "The Lord gives the word" (verse 11).
- *Mighty God:* "He sounds out His voice, His mighty voice. Ascribe power to God" (v. 33-34).
- *Everlasting Father:* "Father of the fatherless and protector of widows is God in His holy habitation" (v. 5).
- *Prince of Peace:* "Our God is a God of salvation, and to God, the Lord, belong deliverances from death" (v. 20).

No where does Jesus ever call Himself the Father. He says that He is one with the Father (John 10:30), but that is not the same as calling Himself the Father. Jesus being one with the Father is believed by all who have an orthodox understanding of the triune nature of God. Anyone who does not believe in the triune nature of God does not know Jesus.

The doctrine of the Trinity is complicated because we're not God. Yet as difficult as it is to get our minds around, the Trinity is an essential part of who God is. To deny the Trinity is to deny something fundamental about God. Yet this is what onenists, unitarians, and modalists do when they reject that God is one God in three persons. They likewise reject the prophets and the apostles who have testified to the glory of God.

The coming of our Lord Christ was prophesied, and the testimony of the apostles is true: "We have seen and testify that the Father has sent His Son to the be the Savior of the world" (1 John 4:14).

REFLECTION

Read the story of Jesus' baptism in Matthew 3:13-17. Who is the Son? Who is the Holy Spirit? Who is the Father? Why is it important to know that God is one God, three persons? Why is it such a serious error to deny the doctrine of the Trinity? If you are studying this book together as a family, take a moment first to pray. Then at the end of your prayer, sing together the *Doxology*.[61] Here are the lyrics:

---

[61] Ken, Thomas. "Doxology" [also known as Old One Hundredth] *(Hymns of Grace)*. Hymn 440.

Praise God, from whom all blessings flow;
Praise Him, all creatures here below.
Praise Him above, ye heavenly host;
Praise Father, Son, and Holy Ghost.
Amen.

Myth #17
"Joy to the World" is a Christmas song.

What do you get when you take "the greatest composer that ever lived" (Beethoven's words) and team him up with the greatest hymnist that ever lived (my words)? You get *Joy to the World,* with music by George Handel and lyrics by Isaac Watts.

Known as the Godfather of English Hymnody, Watts was a protestant Congregational minister in England at the turn of the eighteenth century. He wrote over 750 hymns, some of which are still among the most popular hymns today, including *When I Survey the Wonderous Cross, We're Marching to Zion, O God Our Help in Ages Past, Alas! And Did My Savior Bleed, This is the Day the Lord Hath Made,* and *I Sing the Mighty Power of God.*

None of his songs are more popular than *Joy to the World,* which has the distinction of being the most published Christmas song in the 20th century.[62] But

---

[62] This according to the Dictionary of North American Hymnology (DNAH). https://hymnary.org/node/6445

like Handle's *Messiah*, *Joy to the World* is not actually a Christmas hymn. Watts wasn't writing about the first coming of Christ—he was writing about His *second* coming!

When Watts wrote *Joy to the World*, he had been working on a volume of hymns in which he read into the Psalms all the glory of Christ displayed in the New Testament. The lyrics of *Joy to the World* were inspired by Psalm 98, particularly verses 4, 6, 8, and 9. Consider the similarities of these verses with the lyrics to Watts' hymn:

Psalm 98, verses 4 and 6: "Make a joyful noise to the Lord, all the earth; break forth into joyous song and sing praises! Make a joyful noise before the King, the Lord!"

> *Joy to the world! The Lord is come!*
> *Let earth receive her King.*
> *Let every heart prepare Him room,*
> *And heaven and nature sing.*

Verse 8: "Let the rivers clap their hands; let the hills sing for joy together."

> *Joy to the earth! The Savior reigns;*
> *Let men their songs employ;*
> *While fields and floods, rocks, hills, and plains*
> *Repeat the sounding joy.*

Verse 9: "The Lord comes to judge the earth. He will judge the world with righteousness, and the peoples with equity."

> *He rules the world with truth and grace,*
> *And makes the nations prove*
> *The glories of His righteousness,*
> *And wonders of His love.*[63]

The song came about after Watts had to step down from the pulpit due to his declining health. He hated to resign, only 38 years old at the time, and his congregation was reluctant to let him do so. The Lord Mayor of London and his wife invited Watts, a life-long bachelor, to move into their spacious estate while he recuperated. Watts ended up living there for thirty-six years and during that time completed several more collections of hymns.

Joy to the World was a lyric written while Watts struggled with depression due to his illness. The tune of the song (which you were singing in your head while you read the lyrics above) was taken from Handel's *Messiah* and adapted by Dr. Lowell Mason, another accomplished hymnist. But that composition wouldn't happen until years after Watts' death.[64]

---

[63] Watts, Isaac. "Joy to the World" *(Hymns of Grace).* Hymn 224.

[64] Emurian, Ernest K. *Stories of Christmas Carols* (W.A. Wilde Company, Boston, 1967). Pg. 73-81.

When *Joy to the World* became associated with Christmas is unknown, but how it fit into the theme of Christmas should be obvious. This is a hymn that rejoices in the coming of our King, which is what we celebrate every holiday season. Coupled with music from *Messiah*, which also became a Christmas classic, the song perfectly fits in the catalogue of Christmas carols.

Remember that Christmas is the season of advent, a word meaning the arrival of an important person or event. We continue to celebrate Christ's first advent filled with hope for the second advent. Just as God fulfilled His promise of a coming Messiah foretold throughout the Old Testament, so we know that God is faithful to fulfill His promises for the future.

Christ will return to judge the living and the dead. For those who are in Christ, it will be a day of great joy! Revelation 19:7-8 says, "'Let us rejoice and exult and give Him the glory, for the marriage of the Lamb has come, and His bride has made herself ready; it was granted her to clothe herself with fine linen, bright and pure'—for the fine linen is the righteous deeds of the saints."

For those who are not in Christ, the Day of the Lord is a day to be feared: "The great day of the Lord is near, near and hastening fast; the sound of the day of the Lord is bitter; the mighty man cries aloud there. A day of wrath is that day, a day of distress and anguish, a day of ruin and devastation, a day of darkness and gloom, a day of clouds and thick darkness" (Zephaniah 1:14-15).

Do not walk in darkness for that day to take you by surprise, but rather walk in the light and be ready. "Let us keep awake and be sober," the Apostle Paul wrote to the Thessalonians. "For those who sleep, sleep at night, and those who get drunk, are drunk at night. But since we belong to the day, let us be sober, having put on the breastplate of faith and love, and for a helmet the hope of salvation.

"For God has not destined us for wrath, but to obtain salvation through our Lord Jesus Christ, who died for us so that whether we are awake or asleep we might live with Him. Therefore encourage one another and build one another up, just as you are doing" (1 Thessalonians 5:6-11).

This was the day that Isaac Watts longed with all his heart to see. By the grace of God, he will see it. All the saints—whether they have preceded us in death, or they are still alive when the Lord returns—will be gathered to Him on that day. We will sing the praises of Christ together in a mighty chorus, and it might sound something like, *"Joy to the world, the Lord is come! Let earth receive her King!"*

REFLECTION

If you are studying this together as a family, sing some of *Joy to the World* together. What is joy? What does it mean to have joy? How can we have joy even

139

in difficult circumstances? How does celebrating the coming of Christ at Christmas give you joy? Looking forward to the eventual return of Jesus, how does this hopeful expectation bring you joy? Here are the lyrics to *Joy to the World:*

Joy to the world! The Lord is come!
Let earth receive her King.
Let every heart prepare Him room,
And heaven and nature sing,
And heaven and nature sing,
And heaven, and heaven and nature sing.

Joy to the earth! The Savior reigns;
Let men their songs employ;
While fields and floods, rocks, hills, and plains
Repeat the sounding joy,
Repeat the sounding joy,
Repeat, repeat the sounding joy.

He rules the world with truth and grace
And makes the nations prove
The glories of His righteousness,
And wonders of His love,
And wonders of His love,
And wonders, wonders of His love!

Myth #18
The baby Jesus didn't cry.

The classic lullaby *Away In a Manger* was first published under the title *Luther's Cradle Hymn*, credited to the great reformer Martin Luther. How that attribution was made is a mystery, but modern scholarship is certain Luther didn't write it. In fact, no one knows who wrote it. If you look up the song in a hymnal, it will say the writer of the first two verses is unknown with a third stanza written by John Thomas McFarland.

In addition to the myths surrounding the song's origins, another myth has originated from the song's lyrics. The second verse goes:

> *The cattle are lowing, the baby awakes,*
> *But little Lord Jesus, no crying He makes.*[65]

Somehow this has perpetuated the notion that baby Jesus never cried, even from the moment He

---

[65] "Away in a Manger" *(Hymns of Grace).* Hymn 232.

was born. Then how did Jesus inform Mary He was hungry or needed changed? Did He just pipe up and say, *"Woman, I've got a stinker over here!"* Maybe He changed Himself. Or does being the holy Son of God mean that He didn't poop either?

To the credit of the song's writer—whoever that may be—the second verse is not saying Jesus never cried. At best, we could say some bellowing cows woke up baby Jesus, and Jesus didn't have a fit over it. There's nothing wrong with the line. The song is good. People are silly.

Hebrews 2:17 says that Jesus "had to be made like His brothers in every respect, so that He might become a merciful and faithful high priest in the service of God, to make propitiation for the sins of the people." Jesus experienced life as we experienced life. We know He got hungry (Matthew 4:2), thirsty (John 19:28), tired (Mark 4:38), weary (John 4:6), angry (Mathew 23:13), and even sad.

The shortest verse in the Bible is John 11:35 where we are told, "Jesus wept." This happened in the story of Lazarus where Jesus' friend grew sick and died. When Jesus was told His friend was sick, He said, "This illness does not lead to death. It is for the glory of God, so that the Son of God may be glorified through it" (John 11:4). Soon enough, Lazarus did die. In fact, he had been dead for four days by the time Jesus returned to Bethany where Lazarus had lived with his sisters, Mary and Martha.

When Martha heard that Jesus was coming, she went to meet Him and said, "Lord, if you had been here, my brother would not have died. But even now I know that whatever you ask from God, God will give you."

Jesus replied, "Your brother will rise again."

Martha said, "I know that he will rise again in the resurrection on the last day."

Jesus said, "I am the resurrection and the life. Whoever believes in me, though he die, yet shall he live, and everyone who lives and believes in me shall never die. Do you believe this?"

Martha said to Him, "Yes, Lord. I believe that you are the Christ, the Son of God, who is coming into the world."

Then Mary came to the place where Martha and Jesus were speaking. She fell at His feet and said, "Lord, if you had been here, my brother would not have died!" John 11:33-37 goes on to say:

> When Jesus saw her weeping, and the Jews who had come with her also weeping, He was deeply moved in His spirit and greatly troubled. And He said, "Where have you laid him?" They said to Him, "Lord, come and see." Jesus wept. So the Jews said, "See how He loved him!" But some of them said, "Could not He who opened the eyes of the blind man also have kept this man from dying?

Now as you probably know the story, Jesus raised Lazarus from the dead. He simply raised his voice toward the tomb, and He said, "Lazarus, come out!" and the man who had been dead came out, his body still wrapped in burial cloths. In this miracle, Jesus Christ demonstrated that He had the power over death itself, "for the glory of God, so that the Son of God may be glorified through it," as He said.

If Jesus knew He was there to resurrect Lazarus — if He knew He had the power to raise him up from the dead — then why did Jesus cry? There may be several reasons. Most of all, I believe, it's because Jesus has compassion for us. He didn't cry when He heard the news that Lazarus had died, but He cried when He saw Mary and the others weeping.

Jesus hesitated to return to Bethany so that the glory of God might be shown through this miracle. Lamentations 3:31-33 says, "For the Lord will not cast off forever, but, though He cause grief, He will have compassion according to the abundance of His steadfast love; for He does not afflict from His heart or grieve the children of men."

Another reason Jesus cried is because Jesus mourned over the effects of sin. "For the wages of sin is death," Scripture says (Romans 6:23). The reason Lazarus died is because all men and women have sinned against God, and death is what we deserve. Even though Jesus raised Lazarus from the dead, he would die again. But Jesus raised him to life so many would see and have faith. "I am the resurrection and the life," Jesus said. "Whoever believes in me, though he die, yet shall he live, and everyone who lives and believes in me shall never die."

This isn't the only story in the gospels we see Jesus being filled with sorrow. In Luke 19, we find the story of the triumphal entry into Jerusalem. This is the event we commemorate on Palm Sunday, the Sunday before Easter. Jesus rode into the city on a donkey's colt, as prophesied in the Scriptures, to the shouts of people praising God and saying, "Blessed is the King who comes in the name of the Lord!" In verses 41-44, we read:

> And when He drew near and saw the city, He wept over it, saying, 'Would that you, even you, had known on this day the things that make for peace! But now they are hidden from your eyes. For the days will come upon you, when your enemies will set up a barricade around you and surround you and hem you in on every side and tear you down to the ground, you and your children within you. And they will not leave one stone upon another in you, because you did not know the time of your visitation.

Jesus was prophesying about the destruction of Jerusalem and the temple which came forty years later at the hands of the Romans—exactly as Jesus said it would. *"Set up a barricade"* referred to the earthworks that were set up around the city when it was under siege. *"They will not leave one stone upon another,"* referred to the destruction of Jerusalem's structures, especially the temple which would be completely razed to the ground.

Hundreds of years before Jesus was born, the prophets wrote that He would be hated and rejected (Isaiah 53:3). Shortly before entering Jerusalem, Jesus said to His disciples, "See, we are going up to Jerusalem, and everything that is written about the Son of Man by the prophets will be accomplished. For He will be delivered over to the Gentiles and will be mocked and shamefully treated and spit upon. And after flogging Him, they will kill Him, and on the third day He will rise" (Luke 18:31-33).

In the story of Lazarus, Jesus knew He would raise him from the dead, and yet He wept. In the story of the triumphal entry, Jesus knew the people would reject Him, yet He wept over them anyway. Here we see that Jesus has compassion not only for His friends but also for those who hate Him. Hatred for Christ will result in destruction.

When Jesus mourned over Jerusalem, it wasn't simply because the wrath of God was coming upon them—it was *why* His wrath was coming upon them. They didn't want God. They hated God. After all God had done for them—especially for the nation of

Israel—they made themselves enemies of God by persecuting the prophets of God and the Son of God Himself.

All of this happened according to the sovereign plan of God. As the disciples would pray, "For truly in this city there were gathered together against your holy servant Jesus, whom you anointed, both Herod and Pontius Pilate, along with the Gentiles and the peoples of Israel, to do whatever your hand and your plan had predestined to take place" (Acts 4:27-28).

Even though this was planned and prophesied, Jesus wept for His friends and over those who hated Him, because the Lord is a God of mercy and compassion. As He said to Moses, "I will have mercy on whom I have mercy, and I will have compassion on whom I have compassion" (Romans 9:15).

Galatians 4:4-5 says, "When the fullness of time had come, God sent for His Son, born of a woman, born under the law, to redeem those who were under the law, so that we might receive adoption as sons."

As the carol *Away in a Manger* concludes, may Jesus *"fit us for heaven to live with Thee there."*

REFLECTION

If you are studying this together as a family, sing the Christmas lullaby *Away in a Manger* together. Here are the lyrics:

> *Away in a manger no crib for a bed,*
> *The little Lord Jesus lay down His sweet head;*

The stars in the sky looked down where He lay,
The little Lord Jesus asleep on the hay.

The cattle are lowing, the Baby awakes,
But little Lord Jesus, no crying He makes.
I love Thee, Lord Jesus, look down from the sky,
And stay by my cradle till morning is nigh.

Be near me, Lord Jesus, I ask Thee to stay
Close by me forever, and love me, I pray;
Bless all the dear children in Thy tender care,
And fit us for heaven to live with Thee there.

Psalm 4:8 says, "In peace I will both lie down and sleep; for you alone, O Lord, make me dwell in safety." Knowing that the Lord watches over you, does this help you to sleep in peace? Jesus lived and died for us, and rose again from the dead—how does knowing this give you peace?

Myth #19

The birth of Jesus is a rip-off of the birth of Mithras.

Did you know that Jesus is actually a rip-off of the pre-Christian god Mithras? According to legend, Mithras was born of a virgin on December 25, had twelve disciples, promised his followers immortality, called himself the way and the truth and the life, initiated a communion-like meal, demanded animal sacrifice, died for world peace, was buried in a tomb, and came back to life on the third day!

Boy, that sounds a lot like Jesus doesn't it? The two are practically identical. It doesn't help the case for Christianity that Mithras predates Jesus by several hundred years. Mithras was the guardian of cattle and the waters in Persia and Babylon before the false god was later integrated into the Roman cults. These facts have galvanized skeptics to criticize Christianity for plagiarizing paganism.

Journalist Lee Strobel wrote, "A book called *The Jesus Mysteries*, which promoted similar themes, was named Book of the Year by London's *Daily Telegraph* in 1999. 'The story of Jesus and the teachings he gives in the New Testament are prefigured by the myths and teachings of the ancient Pagan mysteries,' said the authors, Timothy Freke and Peter Gandy. They added:

'Each mystery religion taught its own version of the myth of the dying and resurrecting God-man, who was known by different names in different places. In Egypt, where the mysteries began, he was Osiris. In Greece he becomes Dionysus, in Asia Minor he is known as Attis, in Syria he is Adonis, in Persia he is Mithras, in Alexandria he is Serapis, to name a few.'"[66]

That might sound like a *Huzzah!* for skeptics and a *Hush!* against Christianity, right?

Nope. It's a big pile of *Hooey!*

Any and all claims that Christianity ripped off pagan religions are easily debunked and refuted with solid scholarship. I'm not going to invest the space in responding to every accusation, but let's stick with the comparison to Mithraism.

It's true that belief in Mithras predates belief in Jesus Christ. However, no Mithraic traditions came about until the end of the first century. That means Mithraism as a religion is more likely to have ripped-off Christianity rather than the other way around.

---

[66] Strobel, Lee; *The Case for the Real Jesus* (Grand Rapids, MI: Zondervan, 2007), pg. 158-159.

Mithraism was a Roman mystery cult merely *inspired* by the Persian and Babylonian mythology from which it was taken.

According to the Romans, Mithras was born of a rock—so much for being virgin-born! As for being born on December 25th, that may not be the day of Christ's birth, but it's not Mithras' birthday either. Remember that Emperor Aurelian chose December 25th as the date to dedicate his temple to the Roman sun god, Sol Invictus. In Roman architecture, Mithras was depicted as shaking hands with Sol Invictus. That's his connection to the 25th of December.[67]

Did Mithras have twelve disciples? Nope. None of the pagan gods had disciples (a word that means "learner"). Pagan gods weren't teachers. Did Mithras promise immortality to those who worshiped him? Maybe. But if Mithras worshipers believed they'd receive immortality, how would that be a rip-off of Christianity? Did Mithras call himself the way, the truth, and the life as Jesus did in John 14:6? Did Mithras die for world peace? Was he buried in a tomb and came back to life on the third day? No, no, and no.

Truth be told, almost no liturgy regarding Mithraic traditions has survived. There seems to be only one similarity that is shared between Mithraism and Christianity, and that's regarding the Lord's Supper and the Mithraic sacramental meal. The only

---

[67] Strobel, pg. 171.

reason we know about this similarity is because a couple of the early church fathers, Justin Martyr and Tertullian, wrote about it. They said, "the Mithraic meal was a satanic imitation."[68] The Lord's supper was derived from Passover, not Mithraism.

There have been many attempts to delegitimize Christianity by saying it's a rip-off of this religion or that religion. All such claims are equally absurd. One of the earliest was in the late nineteenth century by Gerald Massey, a notorious fraud in Egyptology. He claimed that the Jesus we worship today is a version the Gnostics came up with from the Egyptian god Horus. Massey said:

> Christian ignorance notwithstanding, the Gnostic Jesus is the Egyptian Horus who was continued by the various sects of Gnostics under both the names of Horus and Jesus. In the gnostic iconography of the Roman Catacombs, child-Horus reappears as the mummy-babe who wears the solar disc. The royal Horus is represented in the cloak of royalty, and the phallic emblem found there witnesses to Jesus being Horus of the resurrection. The resurrection of Osiris, the mummy-god, is reproduced in the Roman Catacombs as the raising of Lazarus.[69]

---

[68] Strobel, pg. 173.

[69] Massey, Gerald; *Ancient Egypt: The Light of the World,* Vol. 2 (London, T. Fisher Unwin, 1907), pg. 752.

Massey's claims were rejected by historians as fringe nonsense with no basis in fact. But these and similar assertions continue to be repeated by atheists and agnostics, thanks in part to a documentary called *Religulous* by actor, comedian, and talk-show host Bill Maher.[70] In that 2009 documentary, Maher said the following:

> Written in 1280 B.C., the Egyptian Book of the Dead describes a god, Horus. Horus is the son of the god Osiris, born to a virgin mother. He was baptized in a river by Anup the Baptizer who was later beheaded. Like Jesus, Horus was tempted while alone in the desert, healed the sick, the blind, cast out demons, and walked on water. He raised Asar from the dead. "Asar" translates to "Lazarus." Oh yeah, he also had 12 disciples. Yes, Horus was crucified first, and after 3 days, two women announced Horus, the savior of humanity, had been resurrected.[71]

But again, these claims were inspired by Massey who has long since been refuted. Maher gave no

---

[70] And you know Bill Maher is a qualified and credible historian, because he's an actor, comedian, and talk-show host, right? Fittingly, he smokes pot in the documentary.

[71] *Religulous,* Dir. Larry Charles, Starring Bill Maher (Lions Gate, 2009), DVD.

sources for his information, other than a reference to the Egyptian Book of the Dead which does not affirm his claims.

According to Egyptian mythology, Horus was born to the goddess Isis, not a virgin woman. There's no mention of Anup the Baptizer or Asar, nor is such an Egyptian name translated as "Lazarus." Horus was not tempted while alone in the desert; he did not travel the countryside healing the sick and doing miracles; and there's nothing about Horus being crucified, resurrected three days later, and then announced by two women as savior of the world.

Maher and skeptics like him will say they won't believe in Jesus without verifiable evidence, yet they'll believe the "Jesus is Horus" myth without verifiable evidence!

The Apostle Peter said of men like this, "They stumble because they disobey the word, as they were destined to do" (1 Peter 2:8). Peter also said, "For we did not follow cleverly devised myths when we made known to you the power and coming of our Lord Jesus Christ, but we were eyewitnesses of His majesty" (2 Peter 1:16).

Unlike the claims of many other world religious and skeptics, the coming of our Lord Christ is not a myth. It is historical fact, verified by eyewitness accounts. Christians do not believe in blind faith. It is the unbelieving who are blind. Jesus has opened the eyes of His followers to see the truth. When Simon saw the Christ-child, he exclaimed in Luke 2:30, "My eyes have seen your salvation!"

REFLECTION

What is faith? (Look up Hebrews 11:1 to help you.) What does it mean to have faith? Where does faith come from? Read 1 John 1:1-3. How does it help your faith knowing that everything we read about in the Bible comes from eyewitness accounts? In John 20:29, Jesus said, "Blessed are those who have not seen and yet believed." How are you blessed by your faith? Sing together the carol *Angels from the Realms of Glory.* Here are the lyrics:[72]

Angels, from the realms of glory,
Wing your flight o'er all the earth;
Ye who sang creation's story
Now proclaim the Messiah's birth:
Come and worship, come and worship,
Worship Christ, the newborn King!

Shepherds, in the fields abiding,
Watching o'er your flocks by night,
God with man is now residing;
Yonder shines the infant Light:
Come and worship, come and worship,
Worship Christ, the newborn King!

---

[72] Montgomery, James. "Angels, from the Realms of Glory" *(Hymns of Grace).* Hymn 222.

Sages, leave your contemplations,
Brighter visions beam afar;
Seek the great Desire of nations;
Ye have seen the Infant's star:
Come and worship, come and worship,
Worship Christ, the newborn King!

Though an Infant now we view Him,
He shall fill His Father's throne,
Gather all the nations to Him;
Every knee shall then bow down:
Come and worship, come and worship,
Worship Christ the newborn King!

Myth #20

Christmas trees symbolize the worship of Thor.

Christmas doesn't officially begin until the tree is up, right? That's the way it was when I was kid. Right after Thanksgiving, the Christmas tree would be raised in our living room, mom would string it with lights, and then all of us kids would decorate. We would grab our favorite decorations, and dad gave the official countdown before hanging that first ornament on the tree.

Dad went to a Christmas tree farm and got a real tree which filled our home with the smell of pine. I remember getting poked by the branches and my arms would break out in a rash because of the pollen and sap. When the holidays were over and the tree was taken down, a circle of pine needles was left behind on the living room carpet. Real trees are so much trouble, I've come to prefer a fake myself.[73]

---

[73] The National Christmas Tree Association reports that about 30 million real trees are sold each year, versus 21 million fake trees. (*USA Today,* December 14, 2018.)

As much as I enjoy rockin' around the Christmas tree, I can't understand singing *to* the tree. But that's exactly what the carol *O Tannenbaum* is—better known as *O Christmas Tree*. It's a song that is sung to a tree.[74] *O Tannenbaum* is a traditional German folk song, as the tradition of the Christmas tree originated from Germany.

Back in the eighth century, a monk by the name of Boniface traveled through Germania preaching the gospel, a dangerous and life-threatening mission. He came to an area occupied by heathens who sacrificed babies to the thunder-god Thor (yes, the same Thor that is today a Marvel comic superhero). Once upon a time, Thor demanded a child sacrifice for healthy crops or else he would strike you with lightning. His worshipers thought they could appease the thunder-god by sacrificing children beneath a large tree they called the Thunder Oak (also called Donar's Oak and Jove's Oak).

Grieved by such barbarism, Boniface resolved himself to cut down the big oak, putting an end to human sacrifice and prove to the people that Thor

---

[74] My wife enjoys her Hallmark movies every Christmas, and this is without a doubt their favorite Christmas carol. Every Hallmark Christmas movie is sure to have a cheesy romantic plot; a sub-plot that has to do with someone's business; good-looking actors, some of whom you might recognize from yesteryear; snow; baking; a Christmas tree farm; and the song *O Christmas Tree*.

did not exist. In a classic story told by Presbyterian minister Henry Van Dyke, Boniface is said to have preached the following:

> Hearken, sons of the forest! No blood shall flow this night save that which pity has drawn from a mother's breast. For this is the birth-night of the Christ, the Son of the Almighty, the Savior of mankind. Fairer is He than Baldur the Beautiful, greater than Odin the wise, kinder than Freya the Good. Since He has come, sacrifice is ended. The dark Thor, on whom you have vainly called, is dead. Deep in the shades of Niffelheim he is lost forever. And now on this Christ-night you shall begin to live. This blood-tree shall darken your land no more. In the name of the Lord, I will destroy it.[75]

Boniface seized an axe and began to chop. Legend has it that while the monk was hacking away, a great wind began to blow and helped Boniface topple the tree. The people were amazed that no harm came to the zealous missionary. There upon the stump of that once foul tree, Boniface stood and preached the gospel.

To remind the Germanic people that Christ was their God and these pagan gods did not exist, he

---

[75] Van Dyke, Henry; "The Oak of Geismar" (*Scribner's Magazine,* Volume X, July-December, 1891), Pg. 686.

pointed to a small fir tree, saying that would be their symbol of new life. It points upward to heaven and its leaves are evergreen, just as everlasting life is given through faith in the Lord Jesus. Boniface told them that worship would no longer be in the wild wood but in their homes, so that's where the fir tree should stand. There would be no more deeds of blood, but gifts of love and kindness.

And that's the story of the first Christmas tree. Early traditions claim that Martin Luther was the first to decorate the tree with lights, small candles which he clipped to the branches. (That sounds like a fire hazard to me, but Luther burned down Catholic monasteries with *sound doctrine,* not with Christmas trees.) Centuries later when the first Germans settled in the United States, they brought their Christmas traditions with them.

Critics of Christmas trees will say it's a pagan artifact that symbolizes the worship of false gods. On the contrary, the tradition of the Christmas tree symbolizes that we *used to* worship false gods, but now the Christian worships Jesus who fills every believer's home. The Apostle Paul said, "Formerly, when you did not know God, you were enslaved to those that by nature are not gods. But now... you have come to know God" (Galatians 4:8-9).

Nevertheless, critics often point to Jeremiah 10:3-4 to make a case against Christmas. Jeremiah says, "For the customs of the peoples are vanity. A tree from the forest is cut down and worked with an axe by the hands of a craftsman. They decorate it with silver and gold; they fasten it with hammer and nails so that it cannot move." What else can that describe but a Christmas tree, right?

Well, Christmas trees did not exist during the Babylonian exile. This passage is very specifically about cutting down a tree, carving an idol out of wood, and overlaying it with precious metal. Then a person is foolish enough to fear the thing they just made and bow down and worship it. No one is bowing down and worshiping a Christmas tree, nor do they fear it (though they might be afraid of getting stabbed with pine needles).

Personally, I don't see the difference between having a Christmas tree and owning a potted plant. If someone is going to be critical for decorating a Christmas tree in one's living room, that critic better not have a decorative flowered centerpiece on their dining room table.

Are you aware that Thursday, the fifth day of the week, is named after Thor? Literally, the name means "Thor's Day." But you think nothing of Thor when you schedule coffee with friends on Thursday. Thor is a non-entity. He doesn't exist. Every day belongs to the Lord: "This is the day that the Lord has made; let us rejoice and be glad in it!" (Psalm 118:24).

Has the Lord not also made the trees of the forest (or the trees of the Christmas tree farm)? Who looks at a tree and thinks, "Paganism!"? That shouldn't be our thought when we see a Christmas tree—which never symbolized the worship of false gods in the first place. It symbolized *the end* of such a practice.

I imagine the sermon Boniface preached upon the stump of Thor sounded a lot like something the Apostle Paul said among the statues of false gods on Mars Hill at Athens. In Acts 17:29-31, he said:

> We ought not to think that the divine being is like gold or silver or stone, an image formed by the art and imagination of man. The times of ignorance God has overlooked, but now He commands all people everywhere to repent, because He has fixed a day on which He will judge the world in righteousness by a man whom He has appointed; and of this He has given assurance to all by raising Him from the dead.

REFLECTION

Idolatry is more than the worship of little statues or big trees. It's the worship of anything other than God. In what ways might we see idolatry in our culture today? How can we keep our trust on God and not place our trust in created things? The hymn that follows may not be familiar to you. The lyrics date all the way back to the 5th century. You can look up the tune on the internet to sing along, or you can just read the lyrics for a time of reflection. This is *Let*

All Mortal Flesh Keep Silence. Here are the lyrics:

> *Let all mortal flesh keep silence,*
> *And with fear and trembling stand;*
> *Ponder nothing earthly minded,*
> *For with blessing in His hand,*
> *Christ our God to earth descendeth,*
> *Our full homage to demand.*
>
> *Rank on rank the host of heaven*
> *Spreads its vanguard on the way,*
> *As the Light of light descendeth*
> *From the realms of endless day,*
> *That the powers of hell may vanish*
> *As the darkness clears a way.*
>
> *At His feet the six-winged seraph;*
> *Cherubim, with sleepless eye,*
> *Veil their faces to the Presence,*
> *As with ceaseless voice they cry,*
> *Alleluia! Alleluia!*
> *Alleluia! Lord Most High.*[76]

---

[76] From the Liturgy of St. James. "Let All Mortal Flesh Keep Silence" *(Hymns of Grace)*. Hymn 215.

Myth #21
Santa Claus.

Of all the Christmas myths, none is larger than Santa Claus. This legendary figure is said to travel the world on Christmas Eve delivering presents to all the good little boys and girls. He rides in a sleigh pulled by eight flying reindeer, which he parks on the roof and enters the home through the chimney. There, like a charitable bandit in the cover of night, he fills stockings with goodies and places gifts under the tree. Then he's back up the chimney and on to the next house.

His workshop is at the North Pole where he and his elves build toys and make delicious sweets. All year long, he receives letters from children from all over the globe, telling Santa what they want for Christmas. He keeps a list of every child, tracking who that year has been naughty and who has been nice.

Santa is depicted as a portly man with a white beard and a jolly disposition, dressed in a red hat and coat with a white fur collar and cuffs. He's been the starring character in numerous films, shows, songs, and commercials. As elusive as he's supposed to be, it's impossible to look anywhere at Christmas and not see Santa Claus.

But before Jolly Old Saint Nicholas became the mythical figure that he is today, he was Nicholas of Myra, a pastor in modern day Turkey. Little is known about Nicholas since few documents have survived from his lifetime. The earliest accounts of the life of Nicholas don't show up until a few hundred years after his death. According to the traditions that were handed down, here is what we know.

Nicholas was born at the end of the third century into a wealthy family and ordained by his uncle to become a priest. When his parents died, Nicholas gave his inheritance to the poor. In his most famous act of charity, Nicholas heard of a man who had three daughters, but the man could not afford a proper dowry for them (a dowry is property or money given by a bride to her husband on the day of their wedding). During that time, if a woman wasn't married and couldn't find employment, she was practically doomed to become a prostitute.

Nicholas wanted to help the family, but he also wanted to save the father from the humiliation of having to receive a dowry from someone else. So Nicholas went to the house at night, and he dropped a purse full of gold coins through an open window.

He did this for three nights so that the man had three sacks of gold, one for each of his three daughters. On the third night, the father caught Nicholas in the act and thanked him for his charity.

This legend has varied over the years with some accounts saying that Nicholas dropped the gold coins through the chimney of the house. Other versions say Nicholas put three individual sacks of money in the girls' stockings hanging beneath the open window. Nicholas developed a reputation for placing gifts in the shoes of those who left them outside the door, a tradition that continues in some parts of the world to this day.

When Diocletian became emperor of Rome, he passed a series of edicts ordering all citizens to comply with the Roman religion. The people were made to sacrifice to false gods and declare Caesar as Lord. When Christians would not submit to these laws, they were either killed or beaten and thrown in prison. This was known as the Great Persecution, and one of those persecuted Christians was Nicholas.

The Edict of Milan ended the persecution in 313 under Emperor Constantine. Nicholas was released from prison covered in his own blood, and when the people saw him, they proclaimed of him, "Nicholas, Confessor!" Even under threat of persecution and death, Nicholas was a steadfast pastor who confessed his faith in Christ and preached the gospel.

In 325, Nicholas traveled north to attend the

Council of Nicea. This was the first ecumenical council of bishops assembled to unify doctrine and come to an agreement over what Scripture said regarding the divine nature of Jesus Christ and the relationship of the Son of God with God the Father.

At the time, a false teacher name Arius claimed that Jesus Christ was created by God and therefore not coeternal with the Father. This teaching is known to church history as the Arian heresy. Arius took to the floor of the council and sang the following hymn:

> *The uncreated Father created the Son*
> > *the beginning of all things.*
> *The uncreated God adopted the Son*
> > *advancing himself as king.*
> *The persons in the Trinity*
> > *do not share equal glory.*

In the middle of singing his blasphemous song, Nicholas came down to the floor and punched Arius in the mouth.

The council went on to draft the Creed of Nicea.[77] The creed affirmed what is said in the Scriptures — Christ's eternal equality with the Father in nature, being, essence, and substance.

Many critics will claim that the deity of Christ was invented at the Council of Nicea. "Nothing

---

[77] Not to be confused with the Nicene Creed, which was authorized in 381.

could be further from the truth," said Dr. Nicholas Needham, lecturer of church history at Highland Theological College in Scotland. "The overwhelming majority at Nicea saw itself as preserving the ancient apostolic faith against the vile innovations of Arius."[78]

And St. Nicholas was a part of it! Listed in the record of attendees to the Council of Nicea on the tenth line is the name "Nicholas of Myra of Lycia."[79] As best as we can tell, that's the story of the real Nicholas. He died in December 6, 343 A.D., and the Catholic church later designated an annual feast day in his honor held on the anniversary of his death.

So how did we get from St. Nicholas to Santa Claus? Some say he's an amalgamation of numerous myths that include the Norse god Odin, the goddess Hertha, the English myth of Father Christmas, the Dutch belief in Sinterklaas, and the European demon figure Krampus. But whatever you've heard about the influence of other folklore, Santa Claus is an entirely American invention.

In 1809, author Washington Irving wrote a satire in which he concocted a false tradition of Dutch settlers venerating St. Nicholas. It was a brilliant marketing scheme to sell his book *A History of New-York,* in which he depicted St. Nick "riding over the

---

[78] Needham, Nicholas; "The Definition of Orthodoxy" (*Tabletalk Magazine,* April 1, 2006).

[79] Wheeler, Joe L.; *Saint Nicholas* (Nashville, TN; Thomas Nelson, 2010), pg. ix.

tops of the trees, in that self-same wagon wherein he brings his yearly presents to children."[80] The book was published on December 6, which was the feast day of St. Nicholas.

Irving's friend Clement C. Moore loved his character and adapted him into a poem entitled *A Visit from St. Nicholas,* more popularly known as *The Night Before Christmas,* published in 1823. Almost every conception of Santa today is thanks to Moore's poem—flying through the sky in a sleigh pulled by eight reindeer, arriving with toys on Christmas Eve, landing on the rooftop and coming down the chimney, filling stockings over the fireplace full of gifts, his white beard, plump figure, jolly disposition, even performing magic.

A few years later, Saint Nicholas became known as Santa Claus. Many parents believe telling their kids about Santa makes Christmas fun and magical. He's also used as a moral figure to threaten children into good behavior: *"If you're naughty, Santa won't bring you any presents this year!"*

All of this seems harmless enough. But I have three objections to making your kids believe Santa Claus is real. First of all, it's a *deception.* You're lying to your kids and setting them up for unnecessary heartbreak. I've witnessed it firsthand—the tears of a child who is told, by a peer or an adult, that Santa

---

[80]   Irving, Washington; *Washington Irving's Works: Knickerbocker's History of New York* (1895 edition), pg. 181.

doesn't exist.

When my grandmother was a girl, a neighbor told her Santa wasn't real. My grandmother went and got her father's shotgun and pointed it in the neighbor's face and said, *"You take that back right now!"* True story.

Another problem with the Santa myth is that it's a *distortion* of the truth. You're bearing false witness about a real person, a brother with whom we as Christians share our inheritance in Christ. Nicholas gave what he had to help others, he confessed Christ and was beaten for it, and he was zealous for sound doctrine. Telling your kids that he's a magic man watching their behavior from the North Pole with elves and eight flying reindeer distributing presents on Christmas Eve and eating their cookies *is not a better story.*

Finally, Santa is also a *distraction* from the gospel. What is the message of Santa Claus? Works and rewards. If you're good, you get stuff. If you're naughty, you don't get things. What is the message of the gospel? You're a sinner, and God gave us the gift of His Son anyway! We must emphasize the gospel to our children every Christmas, and the Santa myth is contrary to the gospel.

There's no denying Santa is everywhere. When your kids ask you what's the big deal about Santa, tell them the truth about a man named Nicholas of Myra, who loved the Lord so much that he was compelled to share that love with others.

In 1 Timothy 4:7, we're told, "Have nothing to do with irreverent silly myths." They don't get more irreverent and silly than Santa Claus.

REFLECTION

In Matthew 22:36-40, Jesus was asked, "Teacher, which is the great commandment in the Law?" Jesus replied, "You shall love the Lord your God with all your heart and with all your soul and with all your mind. This is the great and first commandment. And a second is like it: you shall love your neighbor as yourself. On these two commandments depend all the Law and the Prophets." Discuss how we can love God with all our heart, soul, and mind. How do we love our neighbor as ourselves? Sing together the following hymn, *Good Christian Men Rejoice.* Here are the lyrics:[81]

> *Good Christian men, rejoice*
> *With heart and soul and voice!*
> *Give ye heed to what we say:*
> *Jesus Christ is born today!*
> *Man and beast before Him bow,*
> *And He is in the manger now:*
> *Christ is born today, Christ is born today!*

---

[81] Neale, John Mason. "Good Christian Men Rejoice" *(Hymns of Grace).* Hymn 226.

Good Christian men, rejoice
With heart and soul and voice!
Now ye hear of endless bliss:
Jesus Christ was born for this!
He has opened heaven's door,
And man is blest forevermore.
Christ was born for this,
Christ was born for this!

Good Christian men, rejoice
With heart and soul and voice!
Now ye need not fear the grave:
Jesus Christ was born to save!
Calls you one and calls you all
To gain His everlasting hall.
Christ was born to save,
Christ was born to save!

Myth #22
Hanukkah is Christmas for Jews.

Hanukkah (or Chanukah) is often thought of as the Jewish Christmas. Both holidays occur in winter. They're both on the 25th (Christmas in December, Hanukkah in the Jewish month of Kislev). They're both festivals of lights. They both involve giving and receiving gifts.

At Christmas, the family gathers together, lights the Christmas tree, plays with toys, and eats good food. At Hanukkah, the family gathers together, lights the Menorah, spins the dreidel, and eats latkes. See? They're the same!

But no, Hanukkah is not Christmas for Jews. While Christmas is a celebration of the incarnation of Christ, orthodox Jews do not believe Jesus is the Messiah. Furthermore, Hanukkah has all but lost its religious significance entirely.

The story of Hanukkah begins before the birth of Christ in events that occur between the Old and the New Testaments of the Bible. The Old Testament ends with the Jews under the control of the Persian empire. In the 330s B.C., the Persians were conquered by the Greeks led by Alexander the Great. Alexander wanted to spread the Hellenistic Greek culture throughout his empire, and *Koine* Greek became the common language. This led to a Greek version of the Old Testament called the Septuagint. Establishing a common language also made it possible for the gospel to spread rapidly a few hundred years later.

The Jews submitted peacefully to Alexander and were allowed to continue their way of life. After Alexander died, control of the empire was divided among his four generals, and the Jews came under the control of the Egyptian Ptolemaic Empire. During this period from 320 to 198 B.C., a large Jewish community grew in Alexandria, Egypt.[82]

In 198, the Seleucid (Syrian) Empire to the north of Palestine took control of Syria and Judea under Antiochus III the Great. His son was Antiochus IV Epiphanes, a name meaning "manifestation," for he believed he was a manifestation of the Greek god Zeus. When he assumed control of the empire after his father, he forced Hellenistic Greek culture on the Jews to the degree that if they resisted or practiced their Judaism, they would be put to death.

In the late 160s, Antiochus IV marched into Jerusalem and desecrated the temple. He erected an image of Zeus in his own likeness on the altar and

---

[82] This was likely where Joseph and Mary fled to when they escaped from the wrath of Herod. See pg. 73-74.

sacrificed a pig, which was an abomination. This was prophesied in the book of Daniel as the abomination that makes desolate (Daniel 9, 11, and 12), and it would remain for three and a half years.

Sure enough, toward the end of the prophesied period of time, a revolt was led by a priest named Mattathias and five of his sons, one of whom was named Judas Maccabeus, meaning "the hammer." This became known as the Maccabean Revolt.[83] Judas led a small group of pious Jews in guerilla warfare and succeeded in driving out the Syrians.

In December of the year 164, Mattathias's sons, the Maccabees, and the Jewish army returned to Jerusalem. They cleansed the temple and rededicated it on the 25th day of Kislev. When they went to relight the lampstand called the menorah, they could not find any oil except for a small jar bearing the seal of the high priest. Because it was sealed, they knew the oil was untainted by the Greek's abominations.

One jar was hardly enough oil to burn the lamps for one day. Incredibly, it burned for eight days, lasting just long enough for a new supply of oil to be made. This was considered a miraculous blessing of God and is commemorated during the festival of rededication we know today as Hanukkah, or the Festival of Lights.

The eight-day festival begins on the 25th day of Kislev on the Hebrew calendar. It is observed by

---

[83] 1 Maccabees 1-8 in the Apocrypha.

lighting candles on a nine-branched version of the menorah, also called a hannukiah. A person may light all eight candles on the first day of Hanukkah and then decrease the number of candles lit with each day that passes, or they may start with one candle and gradually increase the number of candles "until, on the last day, he kindles eight lights."[84]

Hanukkah is not one of the Jewish holidays instituted by the Mosaic Law, but it is referenced in the Talmud, which are the writings of Jewish civil and ceremonial law and legend. It is also mentioned in the New Testament in a single place, and this mention is not as a commandment that the holiday must be observed.

John 10:22-23 begins, "At that time the Feast of Dedication took place at Jerusalem. It was winter and Jesus was walking in the temple, in the colonnade of Solomon." The Feast of Dedication is Hanukkah, and this is the only mention of it in the Bible. The passage continues (through verse 30):

> So the Jews gathered around Him and said to Him, "How long will you keep us in suspense? If you are the Christ, then tell us plainly!" Jesus answered them, "I told you, and you do not believe. The works that I do in my Father's name bear witness about me, but you do not believe because you are not among my sheep. My sheep

---

[84] Shabbat 21b of the Babylonian Talmud.

hear my voice, and I know them, and they follow me. I give them eternal life, and they will never perish, and no one will snatch them out of my hand. My Father, who has given them to me, is greater than all, and no one is able to snatch them out of the Father's hand. I and the Father are one."

Often this section of John 10 will be used to say that Jesus celebrated Hanukkah, and so should we. But that's not at all what's being conveyed. We're shown that though these Jews were devout and pious, their hearts were far from God, for if they truly knew God they would have known who Jesus was — the Yahweh of Israel.

Today, Hanukkah is even less about God than it was in Jesus' day. Though many professing Jews desire to be faithful to their heritage, their hearts are far from the One who delivered them out of slavery in Egypt and called them to be a people unto His name. Ironically, Hanukkah, which began as a holiday to commemorate a revolution when zealous Jews gave their lives to preserve their religion, has become a holiday without their religion.

The Jews of today need the same gospel message that underscores Christmas as much as anybody. As the Apostle Paul proclaimed in Romans 1:16, "For I am not ashamed of the gospel for it is the power of God for salvation to everyone who believes, to the

Jew first and also to the Greek."

REFLECTION

In 2 Thessalonians 2:15, the Apostle Paul said to the church, "So then, brothers, stand firm and hold to the traditions that you were taught by us." What would these traditions have been that the apostles taught to the church? In what ways have we lost those godly traditions? How has Christmas, like Hanukkah, been secularized and lost a sense of religion? What can we do to ensure that we don't lose the true meaning of Christmas? Sing together *Come, Thou Almighty King.* Here are the lyrics:

> *Come, Thou Almighty King,*
> *Help us Thy name to sing;*
> *Help us to praise:*
> *Father, all glorious,*
> *O'er all victorious,*
> *Come and reign over us,*
> *Ancient of Days.*
>
> *Come, Thou Incarnate Word,*
> *Gird on Thy mighty sword;*
> *Our prayer attend!*
> *Come, and Thy people bless,*
> *And give Thy word success:*
> *Spirit of holiness,*
> *On us descend.*

Come, Holy Comforter,
Thy sacred witness bear
In this glad hour!
Thou, who almighty art,
Now rule in every heart
And ne'er from us depart,
Spirit of power.

To Thee, great One in Three,
Eternal praises be,
Hence evermore;
Thy sovereign majesty
May we in glory see,
And to eternity
Love and adore.[85]

---

[85] "Come, Thou Almighty King" *(Hymns of Grace)*. Hymn 326.

Myth #23

Kwanzaa is an African holiday after Christmas.

The Advent Wreath is like a protestant spin on the Jewish Menorah. The traditional Advent Wreath has five candles—three purple, one pink (or rose), and a white Christ-candle in the center. A different candle is lit during each Sunday of the advent season between Thanksgiving and Christmas. The first candle represents hope, the second represents peace, the third is the rose candle representing joy, and the fourth is love. The Christ-candle is then lit during a Christmas Eve or Christmas Day service. The Advent Wreath began as a Lutheran tradition, but it has since spread to many protestant denominations.

Today, there are a few churches who, upon finishing up their Advent Wreath, will put up new candles between Christmas and New Years. Rather than purple, pink, and white, these new candles are red, black, and green. They are the candles of Kwanzaa, a secular African-American holiday.

Kwanzaa was created in 1966 by Dr. Maulana Karenga (born Ronald Everett), professor of African studies at California State University, Long Beach. Karenga, a secular humanist, originally meant for Kwanzaa "to give a Black alternative to the existing holiday and give Blacks an opportunity to celebrate themselves and history rather than simply imitate the practice of the dominant society."[86]

The name Kwanzaa comes from a Swahili phrase, *matunda ya kwanzaa*, meaning "first fruits of the harvest." To create his holiday, Karenga drew from African rituals and black national ideology. Each of the seven candles in the Kwanzaa kinara represent seven principles of African Heritage called the Nguzo Saba. They are as follows:

1. *Umoja* meaning "unity."
2. *Kujichagulia* meaning "self-Determination."
3. *Ujima* meaning "working together."
4. *Ujamaa* meaning "cooperative economics."
5. *Nia* meaning "purpose."
6. *Kuumba* meaning "creativity."
7. *Imani* meaning "faith" (in people, not God).[87]

The colors of Kwanzaa are represented in the kinara candles: green represents the fertile land of Africa, black represents the color of the skin of its

---

[86] Mugane; John M. *The Story of Swahili* (Ohio University Press, Athens, OH; 2015) pg. 255.

[87] Nguzo Saba, Official Kwanzaa Website. http://www.officialkwanzaawebsite.org/NguzoSaba.shtml

people, and red represents the blood that was shed in the struggle for freedom. Kwanzaa decorations include colorful art and foods that represent African idealism. Ceremonies consist of showing gratitude to ancestors, drink offerings and feasts, and reading the African pledge and principles of blackness.

Once the holiday grew in popularity, Karenga softened his position on establishing Kwanzaa as an alternative to Christmas, and he encouraged black Americans of all faiths to participate. Still, as much as Karenga wants to insist that Kwanzaa is a secular holiday, it's more religious than even Hanukkah is. Drink offerings, or libation, are ritual offerings to a god or spirit—in the case of Kwanzaa, an offering to the spirit of a dead person.

Kwanzaa is a celebration of humanism, a worldview in which human values and fulfillment are the focus. The humanist proclaims people to be inherently good and moral and insists that we seek strictly secular or irreligious means to solving human problems. The Christian should recognize that this mindset is of the flesh and incompatible with our faith in Christ.

Romans 8:6-8 says, "For to set the mind on the flesh is death, but to set the mind on the Spirit is life and peace. For the mind that is set on the flesh is hostile toward God, for it does not submit to God's law; indeed, it cannot. Those who are in the flesh cannot please God."

James put it this way: "You adulterous people! Do you not know that friendship with the world is enmity with God? Therefore, whoever wishes to be a friend of the world makes himself an enemy of God. Or do you suppose it is to no purpose that the Scripture says, 'He yearns jealously over the spirit that He has made to dwell in us'? But He gives more grace. Therefore, it says, 'God opposes the proud but gives grace to the humble.'" (James 4:4-6).

For the sake of argument, let's say Christmas once was a pagan holiday that became a Christian holiday. Why can't people do that with Kwanzaa? Again, I don't believe Christmas originated from something pagan. But even if Christmas came from, say, Saturnalia (the Roman feast held on December 17), it has since become something completely different. We don't call Christmas "Saturnalia" with Christian themes. Christmas is an entirely different holiday altogether. If the church were to do the same thing with Kwanzaa, it would become something so different, it wouldn't be Kwanzaa.

Kwanzaa's seven principles teach that people can improve their lives by sheer will and determination. Even the holiday's founder hasn't lived up to that. Karenga experienced deep paranoia due to frequent drug use, and he spent time in prison for torturing women, one of whom his own wife.[88] He also started

---

[88] "Karenga Tortured Women Followers, Wife Tells Court" (*Los Angeles Times,* May 13, 1971).

a black-power group called US, responsible for killing two members of the Black Panthers on the UCLA campus in 1969.[89]

The Bible says, "None is righteous, no, not one," and "We have all become like one who is unclean, and all our righteous deeds are like a polluted garment" (Romans 3:10-12, Isaiah 64:6). No matter how good we think we can be, we will never solve the problem of our sinfulness. Jeremiah 17:5 says, "Thus says the Lord: 'Cursed is the man who trusts in man and makes flesh his strength, whose heart turns away from the Lord.'"

Humanistic traditions never unify humans. Titus 3:3-5 explains that apart from Christ, we are "foolish, disobedient, led astray, slaves to various passions and pleasures, passing our days in malice and envy, hated by others and hating one another. But when the goodness and loving kindness of our Savior appeared, He saved us, not because of works done by us in righteousness, but according to His own mercy."

Kwanzaa is strictly the invention of Maulana Karenga, a self-appointed name that means "Master Teacher" in Swahili. He was motivated by racial bitterness and used bits of east-African lore and lingo to lure an audience into his anti-Christian, anti-people rhetoric.

---

[89] Pool, Bob. "Witness to 1969 UCLA Shootings Speaks at Rally" (*New York Times,* January 18, 2008).

In the book *Scam: How the Black Leadership Exploits Black America,* author and radio host Jesse Lee Peterson wrote the following:

> Kwanzaa isn't a celebration of the African harvest; it is a political statement for the establishment of a separate black nation and racial hatred against whites.
>
> When once asked why he designed Kwanzaa to take place around Christmas, Karenga explained, "People think it's African, but it's not. I came up with [the name] Kwanzaa because Black people wouldn't celebrate it if they knew it was American. Also, I put it around Christmas because I knew that's when a lot of Bloods would be partying."
>
> Karenga has explained that his creation of Kwanzaa was motivated in part by hostility toward both Christianity and Judaism. Writing in his 1980 book *Kawaida Theory,* he claimed that Western religion "denies and diminishes human worth, capacity, potential, and achievement." He clearly opposed belief in God and other "spooks who threaten us if we don't worship them and demand we turn over our destiny and daily lives."[90]

---

[90] Peterson, J.L. *Scam: How the Black Leadership Exploits Black America* (Thomas Nelson, Nashville, TN; 2003). Pg. 35-36.

Remembering and celebrating one's heritage is not a bad thing, but Swahili is not the heritage of most African-Americans. To declare Kwanzaa is a celebration of what it means to be an African-American is an insult to black Americans. No one's heritage should be so cheap that their emotions can be manipulated by any felon that comes along using skin color to push his own agenda.

The Apostle Paul wrote, "So then, brothers, stand firm and hold to the traditions that you were taught by us" (2 Thessalonians 2:15). The greatest tradition is faith in Christ, who has made His followers "a chosen race, a holy nation, a people for His own possession... Once you were not a people, but now you are God's people" (1 Peter 2:9-10). No ethnicity is greater or less than another, "for you are all one in Christ Jesus" (Galatians 3:28).

It's unfortunate that Christmas can sometimes be as secular as Hanukkah and Kwanzaa. But the underlying message of Christmas is still the gospel of Christ. Hanukkah and Kwanzaa often elevate man above God. Christmas is about how God became man. Jesus condescended Himself so that we might ascend to where He is!

This is the promise for those who fear God. Jesus said in Matthew 5:5, "Blessed are the meek, for they shall inherit the earth." James 4:10 says, "Humble yourselves before the Lord, and He will exalt you."

Read 1 Peter 2:9-10 (quoted in part above). How are we a chosen race in Christ Jesus? What does it mean to be "a royal priesthood, a holy nation, a people for His own possession"? How were we once not a people, but now we are God's people? Does knowing this make you think differently about how you look at another person who might have skin color that is different than yours? True love and peace are found only in Christ. If you are reading this as a group or as a family, sing the following Christmas hymn, *It Came Upon the Midnight Clear*. Here are the lyrics:[91]

It came upon the midnight clear,
That glorious song of old,
From angels bending near the earth
To touch their harps of gold:
"Peace on the earth, good will to men,
From heaven's all gracious King."
The world in solemn stillness lay
To hear the angels sing.

Yet with the woes of sin and strife
The world has suffered long,
Beneath the angel strain have rolled
Two thousand years of wrong;
And man, at war with man, hears not

---

[91] Sears, Edmund H. "It Came Upon the Midnight Clear" (*Hymns of Grace*). Hymn 246.

The love song which they bring:
O hush the noise, ye men of strife,
And hear the angels sing!

All ye, beneath life's crushing load,
Whose forms are bending low,
Who toil along the climbing way
With painful steps and slow,
Look now! For glad and golden hours
Come swiftly on the wing:
O rest beside the weary road
And hear the angels sing!

For lo! the days are hastening on,
By prophets seen of old,
When with the ever-circling year
Comes round the age of gold;
When peace shall over all the earth
Its ancient splendors fling,
And the whole world give back the song
Which now the angels sing.

Myth #24

Christmas is a pagan holiday full of repackaged pagan symbolism.

"XMESS IS PAGAN!!!!"

That was the subject heading of an e-mail I received from someone who was upset that I had been preaching Christmas-themed sermons (side note: this was not from a member of my church).

The "Christmas is pagan!" myth is not just the cry of arm-chair cynics sitting in their basements believing every conspiracy theory they read on the internet. Even among people who love Christmas, the widespread belief is that Christmas is pagan in origin. Whenever I'm presented with this assertion, I typically respond with one of two comments: "No, it isn't," or "So what?"

Christmas is not pagan in origin—I believe I've established that from the first chapter. It is not a rip-off of Saturnalia or any other pagan holiday (the fact no one can agree on exactly which holiday Christmas ripped off is enough to testify against this myth). Christmas is a Christian holiday—a celebration of the

189

birth of Christ. If that wasn't what Christmas was all about, our secularized culture wouldn't be so afraid of the very name *Christ*-mas!

How could *celebrating the birth of Christ* be pagan? Someone might reply, "Well, that part's not pagan, but Christmas is full of symbolism that used to be pagan!" I don't believe that's true, but so what if it is? Are you a Christian? If your answer is yes, then you used to be a pagan. You, a former pagan, have been Christianized. Christ has triumphed over your paganism.

If it's true that Christmas is formerly a pagan holiday, then the fact that it has been a celebration of Christ's birth for nearly 1,700 years is a triumph I am not the least bit ashamed to rejoice in. Hosea 2:17 says, "For I will remove the names of the Baals from her mouth, and they shall be remembered by name no more." *No one* writes "The Feast of Saturnalia" on their calendars. We get calendars with the name of Christ printed on December 25th. Praise God!

My brothers and sisters, let us not forget the cross—a Roman *pagan* instrument of death and torture that is now the symbol of our victory in Jesus. Through the cross, our Lord God "disarmed the rulers and authorities and put them to open shame, by triumphing over them in Him" (Colossians 2:15).

If someone wants to say, "Christmas is pagan!" so was the cross, and look at what Jesus did with that? In fact, taking something pagan and subduing it to give honor unto the Lord is a practice done throughout the Bible.

At the start of John's gospel, the apostle began, "In the beginning was the Word, and the Word was with God, and the Word was God" (John 1:1). The Greek philosophers believed that impersonal reason gave order to the universe. The word they used to describe this reason was *logos*. That's the same Greek word John used in his gospel for Jesus: *Logos*, or the Word. He's not just *a* word, He is *The Word!*

John went on to write, "The light shines in the darkness, and the darkness has not overcome it" (John 1:9). One of the emerging beliefs at the time John wrote his gospel was Gnosticism. The Gnostics believed that people were inherently good, and everyone had light inside of them. John showed that everyone has sin and darkness inside of them — the true light is Jesus Christ, the One who overcomes the darkness.

In both examples, John took otherwise irreligious concepts and showed how they point to Jesus Christ through general revelation. He took the reader higher than creation — past the created (light and logic) to the Creator (the Light and the *Logos*).

To use a more specific example from the Bible, in Revelation 19, John sees a vision of Jesus riding on a white horse. He wrote, "Then I saw heaven opened, and behold, a white horse! The one sitting on it is called Faithful and True, and in righteousness He judges and makes war" (Revelation 19:11). Many like to use this passage to argue that there are animals in heaven, but that is far from the point.

In Roman culture, when Caesar returned after conquering his enemies, he entered the city on a white horse. This was also because Caesar believed himself to be a god. In Revelation, Jesus returns to conquer His enemies on a white horse. And He doesn't merely think of Himself as God—*He is God*. In John's vision, he took a Roman pagan symbol and Christianized it to show Jesus is greater than Caesar.

There are other places this is done in the Bible, even in the Old Testament. The practice of tithing was pagan before it was Hebrew. Abraham refused to honor a pagan king and instead gave the spoils from war to the King priest of Salem—Melchizedek, who was a forerunner to Christ.[92] Thousands of temples had been built to false gods long before there was a single temple to the one true and living God.

If we're going to dump everything with pagan origins, there are many everyday acceptances we must purge—birthdays, wedding rings, windchimes, potlucks, tattoos, star charts, names of planets, any building with a cornerstone laid by the Freemasons. Every reference to dogs in the Bible is always negative and dirty. Should we not own dogs? Even saying "bless you" when someone sneezes comes from the belief that evil spirits cause illness.

---

[92] Genesis 14:17-24, Psalm 110:4, Hebrews 5:6.

If we're going to get rid of everything pagan, we'll have to throw away the entire calendar. Sunday is named after the sun god; Monday after the moon goddess; Tuesday after the god Tyr; Wednesday after Odin; Thursday after Thor; Friday after the goddess Frigga; and Saturday after Saturn, the Roman god of agriculture. January is named for the Roman god Janus. February is derived from Februa, the Roman festival of purification. March is named after Mars, the Roman god of war... Shall I go on?

By the way, one group did try to do away with the calendar because of its pagan references—the Jehovah's Witnesses. They came up with something called Jehovah's Memorial Calendar, which changed the days of the week to names such as Lightday, Heavenday, and Earthday, and the months had names like Redemption, Life, and Vistment. Needless to say, it didn't catch on. The Witnesses decided the Gregorian calendar was fine thanks to "Jehovah's organization of pagan elements."[93]

Still, the JW's have made numerous attempts to purge the world of things they believe are pagan in origin, including Christmas. The first person to say to me, "Christmas is pagan, and Christians shouldn't celebrate it," was a Jehovah's Witness. But the JW's deny the incarnation of Christ. If you hate things you think have pagan origins and believe that rejecting

[93] Chryssides, George D. *Jehovah's Witnesses: Continuity and Change* (Routledge, New York, 2016). Pg. 320.

such things will make you a better person, should we conclude you're behaving as a Jehovah's Witness?

The "Christmas is pagan" zealots like to quote Job 14:4, which says, "Who can bring a clean thing out of an unclean? There is not one." They say this to suggest Christmas has been made unclean by paganism, and our Christianizing does nothing to make it clean. Since when have pagans been given such authority over days that they're able to make them unclean? Is God not the author of days?

In context, Job 14:4 is about how a man cannot make himself clean — even if a man purges himself of everything that is pagan. Only God, who is holy and without blemish, can make a man righteous. That is what Jesus Christ has done for us. In 2 Corinthians 5:21, we read, "For our sake He became sin who knew no sin, so that in Him we might become the righteousness of God." Jesus took our sin upon Himself with His death on the cross, and He has clothed us in His righteousness, all who believe in Him.

No one is going to fall into judgment because they celebrated Christmas. People fall into judgment "because they exchanged the truth about God for a lie and worshiped and served the creature rather than the Creator, who is blessed forever! Amen" (Romans 1:25).

It is certainly possible to do that with Christmas, but Christmas is not inherently pagan. A person who celebrates the incarnation of the Son at Christmas is most certainly not worshiping the created thing rather than the Creator. Paganism is worshiping created things. Christianity is worshiping Christ.

REFLECTION

Ephesians 4:21-24 says, "Assuming that you have heard about Him and were taught in Him, as the truth is in Jesus, put off your old self, which belongs to your former manner of life and is corrupt through deceitful desires, and be renewed in the spirit of your minds, and put on the new self, created after the likeness of God in true righteousness and holiness." What is the old self? What is the new self? How do we put off the old and put on the new? In the chapter on *Joy to the World*, there was one verse of the song that wasn't included. Sing this last verse together (and you can sing the rest of *Joy to the World* again if you like). Here are the lyrics:

No more let sins and sorrows grow,
Nor thorns infest the ground;
He comes to make His blessings flow
Far as the curse is found, far as the curse is found,
Far as, far as the curse is found.

Myth #25

Christians shouldn't celebrate Christmas.

The late R.C. Sproul was once asked, "Given arguments against Christmas from the reformers, should protestants celebrate Christmas?" Dr. Sproul replied, "I think the Grinch who stole Christmas was an evangelical."[94]

The way some cynics carry on about Christmas, you would think a preacher is prohibited from reading the first two chapters of Matthew or Luke in December. Take, for example, the American puritans. As much as I love reading the puritans, the puritans of old New England hated Christmas. In an early lawbook for the Massachusetts Bay Colony, we read the following:

> For preventing disorders arising in several places within this jurisdiction, by reason of some

---

[94] #AskRC, Live Twitter Event: December, 2016. https://www.ligonier.org/blog/askrc-live-twitter-event-december-2016/

still observing such festivals superstitiously kept in other countries, to the great dishonor of God and offence of others, it is therefore ordered by this Court and the authority thereof, that whosoever shall be found observing any such day as Christmas or the like, either by forbearing of labor, feasting, or any other way, upon such accountants as aforesaid, every person so offending shall pay of every such offence five shillings, as a fine to the county.[95]

At the time, the Massachusetts Bay Colony was a theocracy run by Puritan Christians. In 1659, they actually banned Christmas and made celebrating it a criminal offense.[96]

Why did Puritans ban Christmas? The reasoning is given in their law: Christmas was "superstitiously kept in other countries." Having just fled persecution under the Anglicans in England, many Christians in the new world were sensitive to anything that would be considered either Anglican or Catholic. Christmas

---

[95] The Colonial Laws of Massachusetts: Reprinted from the Edition of 1660, With the Supplements to 1672; containing Also, the body of Liberties of 1641 (Classic Reprint), Forgotten books, March 3, 2018. Pg. 57-58.

[96] My first ancestor to the United States was also a Puritan, but he was kicked out of the colony for rejecting their reconstructionist eschatology and the baptism of infants. He went on to co-found the first Baptist church planted in North America — First Baptist Church of Providence, RI.)

became a blasphemous festival in the hands of those false teachers. The Puritans believed the holiday could not be justified by the holy Scriptures.

Or could it be? In truth, yes—the celebration of Christmas absolutely passes the biblical test.

Now, to be clear, there's nothing in the Bible that says Christians *should* celebrate Christmas. As I said in the opening chapter, Christmas as a holiday is never mentioned in the New Testament. But there's certainly nothing in the Bible that says Christians *shouldn't* celebrate Christmas.

This is no mere argument from silence. We read in Romans 14:5-6, "One person esteems one day as better than another, while another esteems all days alike. Each one should be fully convinced in his own mind. The one who observes the day, observes it in honor of the Lord."

One may argue, "But this chapter of Romans has to do with dietary laws and Sabbath observances!" I agree, that's certainly the context. The Apostle Paul was addressing two very specific issues going on in the church in Rome which had become disputes between Gentile and Jewish Christians. Those two issues were these: were the Jewish dietary laws to be observed by Christians; and which day of the week should be considered holy, the Sabbath (Saturday) or another day?

Paul argued here, as he had in other places, that no food is unclean unless one thinks it's unclean (v.14). Likewise, there's no day that's inherently better than any other. If a person thinks one day is holy, he observes it in honor of the Lord.

So yes, while there are specific issues being addressed, there's a greater principle being applied. We call this Christian liberty: the understanding that Christians are free to receive, with wisdom, anything not expressly forbidden in the Bible. Still, we must be mindful of each other. Just because we are convinced that something is good does not mean we should do it if it might cause a brother to fall into temptation.

A common example of this principle is with regards to the consumption of alcohol. Nothing in the Bible prohibits drinking beer, wine, or other strong drink. However, drunkenness is expressly forbidden. One who has self-control may drink wine. But if in drinking wine they cause a weaker brother to fall into drunkenness, they've sinned by causing their brother to sin. The Apostle Paul said, "Take care that this right of yours does not somehow become a stumbling block to the weak" (1 Corinthians 8:9).

In 1 Timothy 4:4-5, we read, "For everything created by God is good, and nothing is to be rejected if it is received with thanksgiving, for it is made holy by the word of God and prayer."

Are days not created by God? Is Christmas not a day? If received with thanksgiving, covered by the word of God and with prayer, can it not be observed in a such a way that is pleasing and honoring to

God? Of course it can!

Now again, let me emphasize that there's nothing in the Bible that says someone *should* celebrate Christmas. If a person is convinced that celebrating Christmas is wrong, they should not be forced to celebrate it, for they would be sinning by going against their conscience. By the same token, no one can be told that they *shouldn't* celebrate Christmas, for there is nothing in the Bible that prohibits the observance of such a holiday.

What the Bible does say is that every Christian should do is go to church. The American Puritans were wrong to prohibit Christians from gathering in church on Christmas Day, and so is any Christian who, in protest against Christmas, refuses to go to church should December 25th fall on a Sunday.

Hebrews 10:24-25 says, "Let us consider how to stir up one another to love and good works, not neglecting to meet together, as is the habit of some, but encouraging one another, and all the more as you see the Day drawing near." Jesus said, "I will build my church, and the gates of hell shall not prevail against it" (Matthew 16:18).

The gathering of the local church is the institution of Christ. We are His body, and He is our Head. As it says in Romans 12:5, "So we, though many, are one body in Christ, and individually members one of another." Colossians 1:18 says, "He is the head of the body, the church." If you do not regularly attend church, you have separated yourself from the body. What happens to a part of the body that's been cut off from the rest? It withers up and dies.

One negative thing that has resulted from an emphasis on holidays like Christmas and Easter is the breed of carnal Christian called a *Creaster* — that is, someone who only goes to church on Christmas and Easter. Such a person has made these holidays into idols, that God is somehow pleased with them because at least they remember to go to church on Christmas and Easter. But what their sparse church attendance actually conveys is that they don't have any real desire for God or for the people of God.

If you love Jesus, you will love His people, and you will desire to be with His people. Colossians 3:15-16 says, "Let the peace of Christ rule in your hearts, to which indeed you were called in one body. And be thankful. Let the word of Christ dwell in you richly, teaching and admonishing one another in all wisdom, singing psalms and hymns and spiritual songs, with thankfulness in your hearts to God."

Ephesians 5:18-21 addresses the church, "Be filled with the Spirit, addressing one another in psalms and hymns and spiritual songs, singing and making melody to the Lord with your heart, giving thanks always and for everything to God the Father in the name of our Lord Jesus Christ, submitting to one another out of reverence for Christ."

More important than celebrating Christmas is the

regular gathering of the saints to worship God on Sunday, which is referred to in the Bible as the Lord's Day. In fact, when it comes down to it, church is heaven practice. Rejoicing in the Lord for His goodness, glorifying Him for His perfect will, and praising His name in song — is this not what we see the saints doing in heaven for all eternity in the book of Revelation? Church is heaven on earth. Why would a Christian not be ecstatic in heart to attend?

Now certainly, church is full of sinners, and in heaven there won't be a sinner among us. But if the reason you won't go to church is because you don't want to worship with sinners, look in the mirror, for you're one of them. Should anyone not want to worship with you? The difference between a believer and an unbeliever is that an unbeliever thinks he's righteous while a believer knows he's not. We need Christ to cleanse us from all unrighteousness. And that is what He is doing for His church. It began over 2,000 years ago with a little baby born in Bethlehem.

The Christmas story can be summed up in three words: "God with us." This is the name He came to us with: "They shall call His name Immanuel, which means God with us" (Matthew 1:23). This is the promise He left us with: "And behold, I am with you always, to the end of the age" (Matthew 28:20).

God is with us. Believe in His Son, Jesus Christ, and you will have fellowship God and the promise of everlasting life in His eternal kingdom.

Permit me to conclude with the words of Dr. Dustin Benge:

Into our curse,
Into our pain,
Into our distress,
Into our misery,
Into our depravity,
Into our sin,

Enters the incarnate God, Jesus Christ, to make all things new.

Rejoice!

REFLECTION

Thank you for reading *25 Christmas Myths and What the Bible Says*. I hope this book has encouraged your spirit, enlivened you with the gospel, and enhanced your worship of Christ our Savior—not just at Christmas, but every day! What are some things you learned in this book that you did not know before? How has it changed your perspective of the holiday? What's a way that you can use Christmas (or today) to share the gospel with someone else? Select your favorite Christmas carol or hymn and sing it with your family!

Scripture Index

The following is a list of the Scripture references that were used in each chapter. The references are given in the order in which they would be found in the Bible.

1. Jesus was born on December 25.
Matthew 2:16
Luke 2:8-14
John 1:14
2 Corinthians 9:15
Philippians 2:9
1 Timothy 1:15

2. Mary wasn't married when she became pregnant.
Matthew 1:18-25, 13:55
Mark 2:19, 6:3
Luke 1:28-38
John 3:29, 14:3-4
Ephesians 5:22-33
Revelation 18:23, 19:7, 19:6-10, 21:9

3. The gospel of Luke is wrong about the census.
Exodus 30:11-16
Numbers 26:52-56
Joshua 13-22
2 Samuel 24:1-9
1 Chronicles 21:1-17

Proverbs 30:5
Luke 1:3-4; 2:1-5, 3:1
Acts 5:37, 17:26
2 Peter 1:21

4. Mary and Joseph were turned away by an innkeeper.
Luke 2:6-7; 10:30, 22:11
Romans 3:23, 6:23

5. Jesus was born in a barn.
Isaiah 7:14
Luke 1:2; 2:6-7, 10-12.
2 Corinthians 8:9
Philippians 2:3-11
1 Corinthians 15:3-4

6. Angels sang to shepherds.
Exodus 15:1, 20-21
Job 26:7; 38:7
Psalm 13:2, 5-6; 68:4; 89:1; 96:1-2; 100:2; 101:1; 108:1
Isaiah 44:23; 49:13
Jeremiah 51:48
Matthew 25:41
Luke 2:8-14; 21:5
Romans 3:24-25
Ephesians 5:18-19
Colossians 3:16
Titus 2:14
1 Peter 1:10-12
Revelation 12:4; 14:2-3; 15:3

7. Three kings attended the birth of Jesus.
Psalm 72:10-11

Daniel 2:21; 6:3; 7:13-14
Matthew 2:1-12, 16; 27:11-14
Mark 15:23
John 1:11-13; 19:19-22, 39

8. The star the wise men followed was a natural phenomenon.
Numbers 24:16-17
Isaiah 9:2
Matthew 2:1-2, 9-10; 5:14
John 8:12
Philippians 2:14-16

9. King Herod killed thousands of baby boys.
Jeremiah 31:15
Habakkuk 1:2-5
Matthew 2:14, 16
Acts 2:23, 4:28

10. The virgin birth is not important.
Isaiah 7:14
Matthew 1:20-21
Luke 1:35, 37
John 1:29; 8:41
Romans 3:23-26; 5:11-12; 8:11, 17
Ephesians 5:2
Hebrews 9:22

11. Mary the mother of Jesus was without sin.
Leviticus 12:1-8
Mark 10:18; 16:1
Luke 1:42-55; 2:22-24; 18:19
Acts 1:14

Romans 3:23
1 Timothy 2:5-6
1 John 1:9

12. Matthew and Luke's genealogies of Jesus contradict each other.
Deuteronomy 25:5-10
Matthew 1:1-17; 5:17
Luke 3:23-38
Romans 8:15
Galatians 4:6

13. Matthew's genealogy traces Joseph's ancestry while Luke's traces Mary's.
2 Samuel 7:16
Psalm 18:50
Isaiah 9:7
1 Corinthians 15:21-22, 45, 47-49
Galatians 3:29
Ephesians 1:20
2 Timothy 2:15
Hebrews 1:3; 12:2
2 Peter 1:19

14. Mary is the new Eve.
Genesis 3:1-21
Galatians 4:26
John 2:1-11; 4:21
Romans 5:8
Ephesians 5:22-28

15. Jesus was an only child.
Genesis 1:26-31; 2:24

Matthew 2:13-15; 5:28; 13:54-56; 19:4-6
1 Corinthians 7:1-5
1 Timothy 4:1-3
Hebrews 13:4

16. Jesus is God the Father.
Deuteronomy 8:5
Job 12:13
Psalm 33:11; 46:9; 50:1; 68:5, 11, 20, 33-34, 103:13
Isaiah 9:6-7; 28:29
Matthew 3:13-17; 11:27
John 1:18; 10:30; 14:27; 15:26
Philippians 4:7, 9
1 John 4:14; 5:6
Revelation 3:19; 19:6

17. "Joy to the World" is a Christmas Song.
Psalm 98: 4, 6, 8, 9
Zephaniah 1:14-15
1 Thessalonians 5:6-11
Revelation 19:7-8

18. The baby Jesus didn't cry.
Psalm 4:8
Isaiah 53:3
Lamentations 3:31-33
Matthew 4:2; 23:13
Mark 4:38
Luke 18:31-33; 19:41-44
John 4:6; 11:1-44; 19:28
Acts 4:27-28
Romans 6:23; 9:15
Galatians 4:4-5

Hebrews 2:17

19. The birth of Jesus is a rip-off of the birth of Mithras.
Luke 2:30
John 14:6; 20:29
Hebrews 11:1
1 Peter 2:8
2 Peter 1:16
1 John 1:1-3

20. Christmas trees symbolize the worship of Thor.
Psalm 118:24
Jeremiah 10:3-4
Acts 17:29-31
Galatians 4:8-9

21. Santa Claus.
Matthew 22:36-40
1 Timothy 4:7

22. Hanukkah is Christmas for Jews.
Daniel 9, 11, 12
John 10:22-30
Romans 1:16
2 Thessalonians 2:15

23. Kwanzaa is Christmas for African-Americans.
Isaiah 64:6
Jeremiah 17:5
Matthew 5:5
Romans 3:10-12; 8:6-8
Galatians 3:28
2 Thessalonians 2:15

Titus 3:3-5

James 4:4-6, 10

1 Peter 2:9-10

24. Christmas is a pagan holiday full of repackaged pagan symbolism.

Genesis 14:17-24

Job 14:4

Psalm 110:4

John 1:1, 9

Romans 1:25

2 Corinthians 5:21

Ephesians 4:21-24

Colossians 2:15

Hebrews 5:6

Revelation 19:11

25. Christians shouldn't celebrate Christmas.

Matthew 1:23; 16:18; 28:20

Romans 12:5; 14:5-6, 14

1 Corinthians 8:9

Ephesians 5:18-21

Colossians 1:18; 3:15-16

1 Timothy 4:4-5

Hebrews 10:24-25

Made in United States
Orlando, FL
26 November 2022

25063290R00129